S0-DXL-911

JOURNEY INTO FULLNESS

James Mahoney

Broadman Press
Nashville, Tennessee

*This book is lovingly dedicated
to my wife, Betty, the radiant
light God gave to brighten my
path along the way.*

© Copyright 1974　•　Broadman Press
All rights reserved
ISBN: 0-8054-5221-4
4252-21

Library of Congress Catalog Card Number: 73-91615
Dewey Decimal Classification: 248.4
Printed in the United States of America

Contents

THE PLOT

TRAVELER'S AIDS

Read!

THE PLOT

For years Christians have labored under the burden of a great disparity in the Christian life. I speak of the wide gap between the rich promises of God and the contrasting poverty of our spiritual experience. The Scriptures promise so much, while Christians experience so little! It seems there is a Christian credibility gap!

Much of my life was lived on this side of the gap. I had heard so many speak of a "fullness," but my own experience always seemed to lack something. Those over whom I had spiritual watchcare seemed even more empty. Others were, also. Typical of our age, we were all *vogue* on the outside, but all *vague* on the inside!

In all honesty, I got off on so many needless detours, went down so many blind alleys, that I would have ended the journey long ago, as many have, except God kept leading me to higher levels of spiritual living. Each new level of spiritual development inspired me to go on. So I have journeyed ever upward, always looking for that "pot of gold" to appear at the end of some rainbow from whence I could satisfy my longing for lasting contentment.

There is a full relationship with God which satisfies the longing of the soul and neutralizes the appeal of the world! However, to my amazement, I am now discovering that the fulfillment of the quest for spiritual fullness is found in the journey itself, not in some final experience. Through the journey, we reach various, higher levels of spiritual experience. Lasting contentment is found in the journey itself, as we finally reach the last plateau and journey on through upon the level of "spiritual maturity."

God has an abundant life for every Christian. But we must arrive at a level of maturity in our spiritual growth before we can enjoy the fullness of our inheritance as children of God. I want to share my discoveries in how to attain the fullness of God for our lives!

To gain a perspective for beginning the journey, let me provide a "handle." This handle will enable you to get a rational hold on all the vast and varied promises of God. Actually, all the promises of God can be reduced to two. That's right, everything God has promised us can be listed under two categories. God has promised to: save us *from something* and save us *to something*. Ultimately, we will be: saved *from hell* and saved *to heaven*. But, for now, we can also be: saved *from bondage* and saved *to a heritage*. And in this book, we want to enlarge upon all that is involved in these two promises.

A classic example of both promises is found in the Old Testament. It has to do with God's twofold promise to Moses. God promised Moses to lead the children of Israel out of Egyptian bondage and into the heritage of a promised land:

Wherefore say unto the children of Israel, I am the Lord, and I will bring you out from under the burdens of the Egyptians, and I will rid you out of their *bondage,* and I will redeem you with a stretched out arm, and with great judgments (Ex. 6:6, italics added).

And I will bring you in unto the land, concerning the which I did swear to give it to Abraham, to Isaac, and to Jacob; and I will give it you for an *heritage*: I am the Lord (Ex. 6:8, italics added).

Exodus, Leviticus, Numbers, Deuteronomy, and Joshua: five full books of the Old Testament, present this one masterful example of God's two-fold promise. Many other chapters in the Bible make reference to this same experience: Psalms 106; 1 Corinthians 10; Hebrews 3; and 2 Peter 1. Think of it! Rather significant, wouldn't you say?

God promised to rescue Israel from bondage, lead them

through the wilderness, and into the Promised Land. And that pilgrimage affords us an example of our own spiritual journey. In direct reference to that experience Paul made this statement: "All these things happened unto them for examples: and they are written for our admonition" (1 Cor. 10:11).

The "Egypt-wilderness-Canaan" analogy is a much used one. Most often the condition of Israel in Egypt is used to symbolize the life-style of a non-Christian. The wandering of Israel in the wilderness is used to symbolize the defeated Christian who fails to develop in spiritual strength and fruitfulness. Canaan, then, represents a victorious spirit-filled Christian who has really made Jesus Lord of his life.

But the analogy will be interpreted differently in this book. I think the children of Israel in Egypt best represent the life-style of the Christian who lives a self-centered life. The Wilderness represents a Christian who has known what it is to die to his own selfishness and to be filled with the Spirit, but he finds a committed Christian life too difficult and his spiritual growth levels off before he reaches spiritual maturity. Canaan represents the mature Christian with a balanced spiritual life, one who enjoys the fullness of his earthly spiritual inheritance.

The journey of the children of Israel from Egypt to the Promised Land constitutes a historical drama in the sense that a drama is "a series of real events having dramatic unity and interest." The plot of our drama is the journey we will take while seeking to close the gap between God's promises and our possessions! We will view a series of events in Israel's sojourn, drawing implications and making applications for help in our own *journey into fullness!*

ACT 1
Egyptian
Enslavement

Read

Scene 1
The Ruler of Egypt
"Saved, but Enslaved"

The theatrical stage ran across the north of Egypt and eastward beyond the Red Sea to encompass the entire Sinai Desert. Then that stage turned north to include the Holy Land itself.

You are the spectator to the drama. But rather than sit as the curtain rises and falls, you are transported mysteriously by the hand of God as scene after scene unfolds. The curtain rises and lowers, rises and lowers, again and again, as the drama progresses and moves east, then south, and then north.

The drama is real. You recall the incidents from your Bible story days. But before long, you realize that this drama is one of those new types that involves the audience. The truth dawns on you. You are the slave and the wanderer. The journey is your own.

The first scene reflected in Exodus 1:7 is bright and cheerful. The children of Israel are in Egypt, where they are prospering. They were "fruitful, and increased abundantly, and multiplied, and waxed exceeding mighty" (Ex. 1:7). Life is blissful.

Then the curtain falls. When it opens, the situation is reversed. Exodus 1:8 reflects a dramatic change. The children of Israel now are enslaved. Their lives become "bitter with hard bondage" (Ex. 1:14).

The explanation for such a drastic change of events is captured in one announcement: "Now there arose up a new king." All their trouble started here! Like a tyrant, the new king assumed his supremacy (v. 9) and subjected God's children to taskmasters (v. 11). He reduced the children of God to a life of abject slavery (vv. 13-14). Israel fell in bondage to an unsympathetic king.

A pattern of life surfaces here, a pattern which I have observed in the experience of almost every Christian I have ever known. It is this: The Christian experience generally begins with a period of spiritual growth and blessing. Life takes on a blissful quality. At first your life is characterized by a magnificent obsession with Christ. But sooner or later, your initial enthusiasm wanes. Your experience levels off. It becomes routine. You find yourself asking, Where is the blessedness I knew when first I met the Lord?

Has this been the pattern of your Christian experience? The greater question is, Why? But to understand why, you must have a knowledge of your old nature.

The Old Nature

Why does a Christian experience degenerate? Why doesn't it last? I believe the transition begins when a new king arises. You see, inherent in the heart of every man is the desire to be king of his world! This desire is hereditary. It is the most deep-seated, persistent, and powerful desire within you. It is a selfish, self-willed, and self-centered tendency. It is a desire to be king, so that all your kingdom revolves around you. It explains your longing for the spotlight and your affinity for center-stage. Someone called it, "the drum major instinct" — we all want to lead the band!

It is the tendency of human nature to disobey God when his laws run contrary to our own wishes. "Doing every wicked thing that our passions or our evil thoughts might lead us into. We started out bad, being born with evil natures" (Eph. 2:3, TLB).[1] Christians have traditionally referred to this tendency in somber tones as "original sin" or the "depravity of man." These terms simply mean that you are born into the world with a natural bent toward sin. This is a hereditary taint in your character — an evil bias — which made it inevitable that you would sin. The Bible teaches: "Behold, I was shapen in iniquity; and in sin did my mother conceive me" (Ps. 51:5).

Every baby comes into the world with this self-centered aspect in his human nature. I call it the inner tendency to say "I want what I want when I want it." Therefore, there were times when you did what you wanted regardless of what God, parents, or anybody else wanted.

Every baby is "born in sin." As sure as he is born, he will sin. No one has to teach a child to sin. It comes naturally. A baby is born with that self-centered inclination. No one is more self-centered than a baby. He has a mother who feels shackled. The baby demands that his desires be met immediately. The household revolves around him. As he grows up, he retains that self-will. I remember one of my daughters wanting to go swimming one afternoon. Our refusal met with an endless series of outbursts from her which ended in a full-scale storm. She ran to her bedroom, threw herself across the bed, kicked her feet, beat upon the bed with her arms, screamed, and cried herself into a state of stormy rebellion! She wanted her own way. If children were not disciplined, it would be "the survival of the fittest!" Children must learn they cannot do everything they want to do. The rights of others must be considered. Thus laws and rules are enforced, to civilize man.

Inherent in the heart of every man is the desire to be king

of his world. We naturally are selfish. The Bible refers to this
self-centered tendency by various names. Sometimes the New
Testament calls it "flesh" (Gal. 5:24). This word is also used
in reference to the human body in about one half of its uses,
but the context will clarify its use. Sometimes it is called the
"self" (2 Cor. 5:15). Self refers to your selfish tendency, not
to your individuality. Sometimes it is called the "old man"
(Rom. 6:6; Col. 3:9). Some modern versions refer to it as the
"lower nature." "Those who let themselves be controlled by
their lower natures live only to please themselves" (Rom. 8:5,
TLB).

All these terms are one and the same. There is a self-centered tendency which, like a tyrant king, controls the life of
every natural (unsaved, unregenerate) man. An unsaved
man is in bondage to this egocentric tendency. He cannot
cease from sin. He is in some degree a slave to the tendency
within, which screams, "I want what I want when I want it"
(see Heb. 2:15). Therefore, he will do what he wants, regardless of what God wants!

The Bible calls becoming a Christian "being saved" (Rom.
10:9). One thing you are to be saved from is your bondage to
this tyrant king — the flesh — this self-centered tendency
within your soul.

The New Nature

A remarkable thing happens when you are saved. You receive a new nature. The moment you are saved, the Holy
Spirit actually comes to dwell within your life. God gives "you
the power of the Holy Spirit . . . when you believe in Christ"
(Gal. 3:5, TLB). The Holy Spirit enters to renew your human
spirit, the higher part of your inner nature (see Rom. 8:16).
When the Holy Spirit renews your human spirit or higher nature, it is the equivalent of receiving a new nature. Describ-
ing conversion, A. H. Strong says, "We may speak of man as
having a 'new nature.' "[2] Jesus called this being "born again"
(John 3:5-6).

Furthermore, your new nature is renewed after the image

of Christ. The Holy Spirit actually enters your life to re-
produce the nature of Christ in you. As Peter said, you become "partakers of the divine nature" (2 Pet 1:4). Therefore, the Bible speaks of "Christ in you" (Col. 1:27). Christ,
by the power of his Holy Spirit, actually reproduces his nature
in you! The Bible abounds with verses verifying this: Gala-
tians 2:20; 2 Corinthians 13:5; Ephesians 3:17; Colossians
3:11; 1 John 4:4. In truth, you receive the "Spirit of Christ"
(Rom. 8:9-11).

May I repeat? When you are saved, you receive a *new nature*. A. J. Gordon says:

. . . it is the communication of the *divine nature* to man by the
operation of the Holy Spirit . . . as Christ was made partaker of
human nature by incarnation, so that He might enter into truest fellowship with us; we are made partakers of the divine nature, by
regeneration (salvation), that we may enter into truest fellowship
with God.[3]

The Two Natures

If I had my choice of anything I could tell a new Christian,
this would be top priority: When you are saved, you do receive
a renewed, higher nature; but, you do not lose your self-centered old nature.[4] You get a new nature, but you do not lose
your old one. You become the spiritual counterpart of "Dr.
Jekyll and Mr. Hyde."

Failure to understand the dual nature can shatter the faith
of a Christian. For example, let me share the experience of a
young man who was converted in a church of which I was pastor.

Because of a drunkard father, Mike dropped out of school
and ran away from home. Three times he was sent to jail on
separate offenses. After he was saved, however, there was an
immediate change in his life. He began to take on the characteristics of a true disciple. Just as suddenly, Mike disap-
peared from the church for a few weeks. He returned to his
old haunts. This was validated by Mike himself when my
telephone rang about 2:00 A.M. one morning. He asked to

speak with me, and in a few minutes he was seated in my parsonage living room.

Mike resembled a wreck just looking for a place to happen. He had not been able to sleep for days. His body literally shook. His voice quivered. He would slam his fist down on the couch and say: "He just won't leave me alone! He just won't leave me alone!" I thought he was referring to the devil, but to my question he replied: "My problem is God. He just won't leave me alone." I questioned him further and he said, "Well, God won't help me to live right, but he won't let me live wrong."

"Mike," I asked, "what are you talking about?"

"Take tonight as an example," he replied. "I was at a beer party. I picked up a guitar and began to sing for everyone. But while I was singing I came to some lyrics which spoke of love. Immediately I thought of the love of Christ and broke out crying. Having made a total idiot of myself, I threw down the guitar and ran out. You see," he continued, "He won't let me live wrong, but he won't help me to live right."

I said nothing, so he elaborated. "Do you remember a few weeks ago when I went over to that church and gave my testimony?"

"Yes," I replied. "Several members told me God blessed your remarks."

"Well," he said, "I felt like God was leading me in what I said also. But when I finished, I walked over to my seat and soon my mind was flooded with the most evil kind of vile and filthy thoughts. Right there in church, just after having spoken for God, I had such thoughts! I knew then that I certainly must not be a Christian."

At this point, I opened *The Living Bible, Paraphrased* and began reading in Romans 7. I explained to Mike that these words were written by perhaps the greatest Christian who ever lived, the apostle Paul. Then I read verses 15 and 18: "I don't understand myself at all, for I really want to do what is right, but I can't. I do what I don't want to — what I hate. . . .

No matter which way I turn, I can't make myself do right. I want to but I can't"

At these words, Mike took the Bible into his hands. Noticing the modern-styled, paperback cover, he asked, "Is this the Bible?" I explained to him this was a modern translation, but these were the authentic writings of the apostle Paul. So he read on: "When I want to do good, I don't; and when I try not to do wrong, I do it anyway. . . . It seems to be a fact of life that when I want to do what is right, I inevitably do what is wrong" (Rom. 7:19,21).

"Oh," Mike exclaimed, "that's me! Where has this been? That's just like me! I didn't realize it was the same with others."

I told him to read the next verse. "I love to do God's will so far as my new nature is concerned" (Rom. 7:22).

"Yes," Mike said, "that's the way it is. Since my conversion, there has been a part of me that wants to do right. I don't attend your church just because there are a lot of youth there. Since being saved, I have actually enjoyed attending church. Also, for the first time, I have the desire to live a clean life. There is a part of me that is different."

"Read the next verse," I said.

"But there is something else deep within me, in my lower nature, that is at war with my mind and wins the fight and makes me a slave to the sin that is still within me . . . So you see how it is, my new life tells me to do right, but the old nature that is still inside me loves to sin" (Rom. 7:23-25).

Mike came to understand the source of these contrasting desires within his heart. Although he had received a new nature at conversion, he had not lost his old one.

I drove Mike home that night and tucked him in. After placing the Bible on a nightstand at his bedside, I closed the door and walked down the outside stairway. Just before getting into my car, I noticed a light come on in his apartment. Surely he won't go out again tonight, I thought. I quietly walked back up the stairway and peered in through the venetian blinds. He had turned on the lamp and was rereading Romans 7 with a broad smile of assurance spreading across his face. It was so comforting! The apostle Paul had the same problem! When you ask Christ to come into your life, you receive a new nature, but you do not lose your old nature.

This is precisely what Paul was referring to when he wrote: "For the flesh lusteth against the Spirit, and the Spirit against the flesh: and these are contrary one to the other: so that ye cannot do the things that ye would" (Gal. 5:17).

The original Greek word for "lust" here is the strongest possible word for desire in the Greek vocabulary. The verse is saying: "The spirit renews your higher nature from which it seeks, with the strongest possible kind of desire, to shut out the influence of your self-centered flesh (old nature). On the other hand, with the strongest possible kind of desire, the flesh (old nature) wants to hinder and nullify the influence of the spirit (new nature). These are contrary one to the other, so that you will find you cannot become the Christian you were saved to be" (Amplified Bible).

Your temporal life will be marked by the conflict of two inner natures that will always be vying for control of your life. We could call them Dr. Spirit and Mr. Flesh!

Some have asked, "If the old nature is not eradicated at conversion, what does the following verse mean?" "Therefore if any man be in Christ, he is a new creature: old things are passed away; behold, all things are become new" (2 Cor. 5:17).

This verse does not say the old nature passes away. It teaches that old things pass away. Your relationship to things will change; some formerly important things will now appear less important, such as material things. Some formerly insignificant things will now appear significant, such as prayer and church. This verse simply states that you become a "new creation" (Amplified Bible) when you yield to Christ's rule in your heart, which will alter your relationship to some things!

Nearly all Christians will testify to a regenerating and revitalizing change in life-style which accompanied their conversion. For a varied period of time, they evidenced a new life.

But I have observed them as their devotion wanes. Most would now admit that Christ is no longer Lord, really in control of their lives. Just like God's children in Egypt, there has arisen a new king in their hearts. Self is back on the throne. They are saved but enslaved. That is the condition of most church members I know!

As the curtain closes on this scene, the children of God are "groaning beneath their burdens, in deep trouble because of their slavery" (Ex. 2:23, TLB)!

Notes

1. Scripture quotations marked "TLB" are taken from *The Living Bible, Paraphrased* (Wheaton: Tyndale House Publishers, 1971) and are used by permission.

2. A. H. Strong, *Systematic Theology* (Valley Forge, Pa.: Judson Press), p. 824.

3. A. J. Gordon, *Two-Fold Life,* p. 22.

4. Technically, a man has only one nature, not two. He is not naturally schizophrenic. He has a higher and lower aspect of his one nature. But for clearer understanding, I prefer to retain the terminology of the spiritual "divines" of old, who for simplicity and clarity, spoke of two natures.

Scene 2
The Residents of Egypt
"What Is a Child Like You Doing in a Place Like This"

The curtain rises again. The general setting is the same. You are in Egypt. But this time, the stage is almost enshrouded with darkness. One central scene is spotlighted.

The scene reveals the hot, sultry atmosphere of the Egyptian brick kilns. Fires rage within the kilns. The heat is sweltering. It is the smoke which belches from these furnaces that darkens the outskirts of the stage. It is also the light from their open doors that illuminates the activities around the kilns, serving as natural footlights for all that takes place there.

Sweat-covered backs glisten in the reflected glow. You are witness to the enforced slavery of the children of Israel as they trudge through their daily grind. Both men and women are engaged in the toil of brick-making. Demanding taskmasters hover over them to enforce a daily quota. The Israelites break forth in occasional song, voicing their burden in mournful chorus, in cadence with their work. You are there to survey the conditions of Israel's bondage!

The children of Israel are in a desperate state. Their position is perilous. Several things stand out. (1) Their service is rigorous: "All their service, wherein they made them serve, was with rigour" (Ex. 1:14). (2) Their sorrow is constant: "And the Lord said, I have surely seen the affliction of my people which are in Egypt, and have heard their cry by reason of their taskmasters; for I know their sorrows" (Ex. 3:7). (3) Their sacrifice has ceased: They were no longer able to withdraw and "sacrifice to the Lord our God" (Ex. 3:18). (4) Their situation is confusing: "Then the officers of the children of Israel came and cried unto Pharaoh, saying,

Wherefore dealest thou thus with thy servants" (Ex. 5:15). (5) Their Spirit is crushed: "But they hearkened not unto Moses for anguish of spirit, and for cruel bondage" (Ex. 6:9).

Egypt became a place of bitter enslavement and fruitless toil. Think of it! These were God's children, subjected to a humiliating bondage. Surely they evoked but one reaction: what is a child like you doing in a place like this?

Perhaps all of us need to "locate" ourselves. How about you? Where is your life in terms of spiritual development? Are you in spiritual Egypt? Perhaps you need to check yourself against the characteristics just mentioned. Take your time. Stop and think as you consider your life.

(1) Is your service coerced? Do you serve out of a sense of duty, or do you really enjoy serving the Lord? Have you gained that effortless, spontaneous enjoyment of serving Christ in the power of his Spirit, or do you serve in your own strength? Is your life spiritually fruitless? Are you "weary in well doing" or do you welcome opportunities to serve (Gal. 6: 9,10)?

(2) Is your sorrow constant? A normal Christian experience is the most joyful life on earth! Be honest. Does your spiritual experience bring joy or sorrow to your life? Do you inwardly complain of what is required of you as a Christian? Is Bible study boring? Is group prayer a drudgery? Do you enjoy the fellowship of other Christians? Does your Christian experience bring constant joy to your life or is it all rather burdensome?

(3) Has your sacrifice ceased? Have you become so selfish that sacrifice comes hard? What are you doing that you would not be doing if you were not a Christian? What are you "giving up" for your Lord? Do you balk at tithing? Do you go the "second mile" for Christ? Are you one of those who says, "Don't expect to see me at church every time the doors open"? Do you maintain a daily habit of Bible study and prayer? Are you rather preoccupied with personal interests at home, at school, or at work? Do you feel a little uneasy around a sacrificial Christian? Do you call him a "fanatic"?

(4) Is your situation confusing? Are you confident about your relationship with God? Are you certain you are fulfilling his wishes for your life? Are you caught in a web of confusing circumstances? Are you right now wondering why God has allowed certain things to happen? Has God let you down? Does he seem a million miles away? Do you recognize the hand of God in your life?

(5) Is your spirit crushed? Are you expecting great things from God? Are you highly optimistic about your Christian life? Are you zealous? Do you expect great things from God, or do you doubt his promises? Have you been hurt as a Christian? Have you become despondent? Are you defeated? Are you anxious and concerned? Are you frustrated in your Christian experience? Have you lost your spiritual drive?

Do these questions reveal that you may be living in spiritual Egypt? Egypt is out of bounds for God's children! What is a child like you doing in a place like this? It is unnatural!

Such Slavery Is Unnatural

The most unnatural thing in the world is a Christian who lives in a state of enslavement to himself. Indeed, you become a Christian by banishing self from the throne of your life and naming Christ Lord. Lord means boss, or master, the controlling figure of your life. The Bible calls this being saved. You could not have been saved had you been unwilling to make Christ Lord!

Dr. David Haney in *The Idea of the Laity* made a weighty observation:

The emphasis of the Church today is on the *Saviorhood* rather than the *Lordship* of Christ, an interesting reversal of the Biblical emphasis. Likewise, we tend to view Christ as Savior as the *cause;* and Lordship as a possible, but not necessary, *effect.* Biblically, however, Lordship is the cause and salvation is the effect! One is saved because Christ is named Lord; salvation is a *consequence.*

"But what does it say? The word is near you, on your lips and in your heart (that is, the word of faith which we preach); because, if you confess with your lips that Jesus is Lord and believe in your heart that God raised him from the dead, you will be saved (Rom. 10:8-9, RSV).

Interestingly enough, the word "Savior" is used 24 times in the New Testament, and only one is singular; all of the other references are plural: *our* Savior, etc. Salvation is more viewed as a *group* phenomenon."[1]

Dr. Haney draws attention to the fact that the word *Savior* is used only 24 times in the New Testament while the word *Lord* is used 644 times. It is quite striking to see this comparison in a concordance. In one concordance, each page has two columns. It only takes about one half of one column of a page to list the uses of *Savior* in the Bible. It takes 51 full pages to list all the uses of the word *Lord*. By sheer weight of emphasis it seems that one cannot merely accept Jesus as Savior. One must accept his lordship, and salvation is a result — an effect.

Christ died on the cross to pay for our sins (Rom. 5:8). However, we cannot accept what Christ did for us apart from accepting him. Else it would be like saying, "Jesus, we'll let your death be payment for our sins — but we don't want you in our lives."

"To hear some people tell it, you can have Christ as your Savior, but the Devil for your Lord. This cannot be. There can be no saving grace emanating from Jesus Christ except by and through an acknowledgment of his Lordship. To believe in a redemptive way means to acquire a Lord."[2]

"For to this end Christ both died, and rose, and revived, that he might be Lord" (Rom. 14:9). No, you cannot accept what Jesus did for you, apart from accepting him — and Jesus cannot be anything else than what he is. He is Lord! Therefore, you must accept him as Lord — and Lord means "boss!"

The secret of a victorious Christian life is maintaining that lordship! This points out the greatest deficiency in Christians today. Jesus is not Lord! Some claim him as Savior who have refused him as Lord. Thinking they are on the journey, they have not even begun. They are unsaved. Others have accepted him as Lord, only to let self regain the throne of their lives. They are saved but enslaved. Together, these two groups make up the majority of our church membership, and their common address is "spiritual Egypt."

Such Slavery Is Unnecessary

There is a sad thing about the children of Israel who suffered that Egyptian enslavement. The previous generation put them there (Ex. 1:6). Their captivity was a legacy. They did not realize they had a promise of deliverance (Gen. 50:24) or that they were mightier than the Egyptians (Ex. 1:9) and could certainly have escaped (Ex. 1:10). Think of it. They could have come out of their slavery but did not know it! Mark it down: If a new Christian received the proper care and directions, he might never fall captive in spiritual Egypt. The whole trip is unnecessary!

Yet, almost every Christian has experienced a long period of Egyptian enslavement following conversion. It seems that you receive Christ as Lord and live obediently for a while. But sooner or later you enter a long period of rather fruitless spiritual existence when you take back the control of your life — to live for yourself. Jesus is no longer Lord. As mentioned in the last chapter, in spiritual Egypt you are saved but enslaved to a stubborn self-will.

Some have drifted into a life of self-indulgence. They have gone the way of the prodigal son who "took his journey into a far country, and there wasted his substance with riotous living" (Luke 15:13).

Others continue to live basically "good" lives — morally, but theirs is a life of self-righteousness. Many of those who continue living "good" lives wake up one day to realize they are living in their own strength, by their own abilities. Indeed, most have not even realized it. They are wise enough to side-step the consequences of an immoral life but have tried to live a "good Christian life" in their own strength. This is self-righteousness! They are still doing "their own thing," but in the church and in utter self-sufficiency. Do you see it? Even their "good lives" operate from a self-centered principle. Some call it serving God "in the flesh!"

Whether it is a life of self-indulgence or a life of self-righteousness, it is still *slavery,* because self is enthroned and the Lord ignored!

But if new Christians receive the proper care from those who lead them to Christ, many would not turn away to live ungodly lives. God is going to judge the church for "child neglect!" If new Christians received deeper instruction in spiritual principles, many would also be saved from self-righteousness. But the moment we are converted, some Christian leader tells us to merely "roll up our sleeves, get out there, go to work for God, and show him how much you love him." We have done just that! We have gone to work for God, knowing nothing of how to let God work through us. Thus, we serve God in the flesh, and what work is allowed to stand is done in spite of us.

very good!

For the most part, our philosophy of Christian service and our Christian life-style is based on a faulty premise! For example, suppose I experience salvation and join a church. I learn a number of things are expected of me. There are some things I am to do. There are some things I am not to do. But these do's and don'ts are based alike on the same faulty premise. They are based on the premise "I can."

I am challenged to attend church, to read my Bible, to pray, to visit, to forego sinful pleasure, to stay away from questionable places, to be an example, to take an active part, to tithe, to witness — and all of this is based upon the assumption that "I can" do it, but "I can" is a gateway to spiritual Egypt!

If I love the Lord enough to do all this, I enter the "*I* will do it" syndrome. In the very process of doing it for Jesus, I prevent him from doing it through me. I begin to live in the "flesh." I blindly pass right by his offer to empower me for service, all the while saying, "I will do it for you, Jesus." As I do things for God, my life begins to revolve around me. I become self-centered through the actual practice of my Christian experience.

Preachers are always speaking on "the seven last words from the cross." Somebody ought to preach on "the seven last words from the flesh," which are: "I will do it for you, Jesus." If I spoke on this subject, I would arrange my sermon in the form of an acrostic, to reveal the subtle self-centeredness behind those seven words:

Great!

I	— by my own abilities and energies,
will	— for my glory,
do	— because good works make me feel good,
it	— because I don't mind this task,
for	— Lord, you just stand aside,
you	— because you need my help,
Jesus	— aren't you fortunate to have me!

Think through it. Once I accept this "I can" premise it becomes the basis for my activity. As an "I can" Christian, I might spend years trying to fulfill all those do's and don'ts! I enter a treadmill of endless activity, always busy — going nowhere. The fact is, once I enter the "I can" syndrome, God will never be able to accomplish his greatest work in me until I experience enough defeat to finally say, "I cannot!"

This explains why most Christians come into the fullness of spiritual victory from a context of personal despair. The self-sufficient "I can" must be shattered before realizing "I can't." Sometimes that takes years.

One friend of mine was thirty-one years of age and pastor of a large church before he really experienced God's control of his life. So weary of struggling to live godly in his own strength, he retired to his study one day and prayed something like this: "Dear Lord, you know my soul longs for more of your life, but I never seem able to live it. Week after week I tell people there is joy unspeakable and a peace that passes understanding in Christ. Well, Lord, where is mine?"

From an honest heart, this prayer went on for months. But his burden only grew more heavy. Finally, his prayer became desperate. "Lord, I have come to the settled persuasion that either the Christian life is not all you say it is or there is something I don't know. Lord, as much as I love you, I have to be honest with myself and quit preaching, or you must reveal to me something I have never known."

At this point of desperate desire one Saturday afternoon he picked up a book his wife had been encouraging him to read. It was entitled *They Found the Secret,* a book of twenty biographies of men who found a deeper experience with God than they had ever known. The first chapter was entitled, "The Exchanged Life." He read a few pages, paused, and a thought struck him with the force of a thunderbolt: How does a branch bear fruit, simply by abiding in the vine! Suddenly he saw himself as a miserable, withered branch, trying to produce in himself what only God could produce in him. That one thought opened up new vistas of spiritual discovery which transformed his message, his ministry, and his manner of life. God broke through his self-sufficiency and took possession of his life. Today he is a powerful pastor of the largest downtown church in one of America's leading cities!

Only from the perspective of "I can't," can you learn "he can." The Bible does teach you can do all things, but only in as much as you are strengthened by him: "I can do all things through Christ which strengtheneth me" (Phil. 4:13).

It is tragic that some do not learn this immediately upon becoming a Christian. At separate times, both Reese Grey and Sonny Lollerstadt were added to the Richard Hogue crusade team. They joined the team while they were new Christians. But they were carefully nurtured in spiritual things. In less than two years each life developed into a deep powerful witness of Christ. However, they came to Christ from a strong Christian background, and from the first the team helped them live by the principles of a Christ-filled life. They have never known a long period of Egyptian enslavement!

The enslaved Christian life is both unnatural and unnecessary. What about you? Do you live in spiritual Egypt?

This scene has depicted the slavery of God's children in Egypt. For all who have recognized themselves there, the curtain slowly closes while an ominous voice is heard from heaven, saying: "What is a child like you doing in a place like this?"

Notes

1. David Haney, *The Idea of the Laity* (Grand Rapids: Zondervan Publishing House, 1973).

2. Culbert G. Rutenber, *The Reconciling Gospel* (Valley Forge, Pa.: Judson Press, 1960), p. 165.

Scene 3
The Release From Egypt
"Take Two Giant Steps"

The curtain rises to reveal a scene of majestic beauty. You are in the throne room of the great palace of Egypt. It is a vast, central hall at the end of a colonnaded court; a room of splendid beauty and dignity. The walls are of carefully inlaid brick. The roof is of imposing, wooden beams.

At the center is an exquisitely decorated ramp leading up to the grand throne. The ramp itself is an inlaid fresco of brilliant design. The throne is surrounded by gigantic columns — almost thirty feet high. The capitals and bases of the columns are decorated with blue and gold petals. The columns boast carvings depicting occasions of historic significance. They are highly decorative, bearing the typically Egyptian motif of papyrus, lotus bud, and flower. The room is softly lighted from upper windows high on the walls.

Seated on the throne is the Egyptian pharaoh, or king. His shoulders and chest are bare, his body bronzed. His kilt has a sunburst of pleats spreading from the lower hem toward the waist, indicating the rays of the sacred sun. He proudly wears the artificial beard, badge of Egyptian royalty. His crown is a high, cone-shaped headdress. Seated upon his throne, he towers above those who stand before him — an imposing figure.

This Pharaoh is the greatest military conqueror in all Egyptian history. He is also a mighty builder. He has constructed cities and a massive temple, using thousands of captives to do his work.

The princess and several women in waiting enter the room to sit near Pharaoh. The high priest, bold and hawklike, is pacing about behind the throne. Soldiers are standing defiantly along both sides of the hall. They are dressed in short, flounced kilts with dagger and sword at their belts, and helmets of burnished copper. Some of them brandish long spears.

Pharaoh strikes upon the floor with an enormous scepter, shaped like a lion's claw. Silence falls and the chamberlain mounts one step and cries in a loud voice, "Oh King, you have seen fit to grant audience to the new representative of the Israelite slaves."

Standing before Pharaoh is a man whose name is to become legend: Moses! He is there as heavenly emissary. He has come to issue a divine summons to Pharaoh, King of Egypt. Moses is to present Pharaoh with this ultimatum: "Thus saith the Lord . . . let my people go" (Ex. 5:1). Pharaoh had to learn who was Lord.

Moses keeps his date with destiny, appears before Pharaoh, and presents the Lord's demand (Ex. 3—4). Pharaoh's response is classic. It is as if he voices the question of lost mankind. He asks: "Who is the Lord, that I should obey?" (Ex. 5:2).

The book of Exodus revolves around that question. The freedom of Israel hung in the balance upon that same question. Indeed, that is the central question of the entire Bible. It is the one great question of life!

The Old Testament presupposes this question in declaring: "The Lord is God." This pronouncement is God's greatest revelation to man (Gen. 2:4; 15:2,8; 28:13,21). God's greatest act of the Old Testament was to make a nation out of those who were "not a people" (1 Pet. 2:10) and all of this was to reveal that the Lord was and is God.

For ask now of the days that are past, which were before thee, since the day that God created man upon the earth, and ask from the one side of heaven unto the other, whether there has been any such thing as this great thing is? . . . God assayed to go and take him a nation from the midst of another nation . . . that thou mightest know that the Lord he is God, there is none else beside him (Deut. 4:32-35).

Elijah drew a line, asked the same question, and called for

a decision: "And Elijah came unto all the people, and said, How long halt ye between two opinions? If the Lord be God, then follow him" (1 Kings 18:21).

This was still the issue in the days of Jeremiah (Jer. 16:21) and at the end of the Old Testament (Hos. 2:20; Joel 2:27; Amos 4:13; Mic. 4:5; Zech. 13:9; Mal. 1:6).

The New Testament declares that Christ is Lord. Lordship is the critical question. Jesus asked the disciples: "Whom do men say that I am?" (Mark 8:27). The full answer to this question was declared at Pentecost: "God hath made that same Jesus, whom ye have crucified, both Lord and Christ" (Acts 2: 36). This was the one question Paul asked at his conversion, "Who art thou Lord?" (Acts 9:5). Indeed, our confession of Christ as Lord is the means of salvation (Rom. 10:9). It is God's intention "that every tongue should confess that Jesus Christ is Lord, to the glory of God the father" (Phil. 2:11).

In defining the word "Lord," William Barclay points out that, in New Testament days, the word "Lord" carried with it an atmosphere of sovereign authority. It was used to describe the authority of the father over a family. It was the regular word for a master, as opposed to a slave. It was a word used to describe the undisputed owner of any property. It was used to describe a military commander. It became the standard and official title of the Roman emperors. In the East it became the standard title for every god. Deissman referred to it as "a divine predicate intelligible to the whole eastern world."[1] So, Lord means boss, master, owner, commander, or God!

The Old Testament declares that the Lord is God, and the New Testament declares Christ is Lord. Lord is the key word. This is the pivotal question of the Bible: "Who is the Lord, that I should obey?"

In Exodus, the question was answered quickly. The Lord gained obedience by twice demonstrating his sovereignty. Exodus records two things God did to prove he was Lord.

A Demonstration of Death

From the beginning, God explained his first demonstration

to Moses. Moses was commissioned to confront Pharaoh. Before Moses went, God predicted the outcome. Moses would tell Pharaoh of the Lord's demand: "Let my people go." Pharaoh would refuse. God would then send pestilence and Pharaoh would seem to give in; then Pharaoh's heart would harden. He would refuse again. But, at the last, God would bring a final judgment of death upon him (Ex. 4:21-23). God himself revealed the judgment of death was the means he used that "the Egyptians shall know that I am the Lord" (Ex. 7:5).

God sent nine preliminary judgments upon the land in order to put down everything the Egyptians were worshiping as God. He executed judgment against "all the gods of Egypt" (Ex. 12:12). Archaeologists have revealed how the plagues were aimed at the gods of Egypt.

1.   The first plague: It turned the water of the river Nile into blood. This was directed at the god Nilus, for the river Nile was worshiped as the god of nourishment and life. But the plague made the water unusable.

2.   The second plague: The multiplication of frogs intended to insult the goddess Hekt, who was frog-headed. With frogs everywhere, the people would soon despise the very sight of them.

3.   The third plague: The plague of lice was aimed at the priests of Egypt, who were careful not to wear woolen garments but only linen to avoid vermin.

4.   The fourth plague: The swarms of scarab beetles were directed at the worship of the god Khephera. Beetles were everywhere — yet the people did not dare kill them, for they represented deity.

5.   The fifth plague: Murrain on the cattle was directed against the animal worship which was so prevalent in Egypt.

6.   The sixth plague: The plague of boils was against the god Imhotep, the god of healing science, who proved helpless to heal the afflicted.

7.   The seventh plague: The hail was intended for the gods of Reshpu and Oetesh who were thought of as controlling the natural elements.

8. ·The eighth plague: The plague of locusts was aimed at a large number of Egyptian gods who were worshiped to insure good crops.

9. The ninth plague: The plague of darkness was to put down the god AmenRa, who was supposed to be god of the sun.

10. · The final plague: Death to the first born was directed especially against Pharaoh himself, since there was an official fiction that the first born son of Pharaoh was an incarnation of the god Ra, and was supposed to have life that was humanly indestructible.[2]

After God pronounced the judgment of death, Pharaoh once again entered his throne room to announce an official decree. God was obeyed as Lord. Israel was set free!

A Demonstration of Power

However, the children of Israel had no more than escaped Egypt when Pharaoh rose up again and sent his armies in pursuit to bring them back! This provided the occasion for the second manner in which God acted "that the Egyptians might know that I am Lord" (Ex. 14:4).

God's children found themselves with the Red Sea before them and Pharaoh's armies behind them. They seemed helpless! Then God demonstrated his miraculous power. At God's word, Moses lifted up his rod and stretched it over the sea: "And the Lord caused the sea to go back by a strong east wind all that night, and made the sea dry land, and the waters were divided" (Ex. 14:21). The miracle was not in the sea but in the wind! Remember this: The force of God's mighty wind divided the sea, and the children of Israel walked through on dry land. The wind ceased at morning, and the waters rolled back to catch Pharaoh's armies in pursuit and drown them.

This was the second step God took to deliver his children from Egypt and these two steps mark the way for you! These two steps represent the drastic measures *you* must take to gain release from your own self-will!

Two Giant Steps

"Who is Lord, that I should obey him?" That is the question.

Are you obedient to Christ? Or, like so many Christians, are you captive to the selfish urge to do what you want when you want? Who reigns as Lord of your life? your Savior or your self? Are you saved, but enslaved? Do you reside in spiritual Egypt?

You escape by the way of an established lordship: That is, you take Christ into your daily routine of living and introduce him as Lord of every situation. Christ wants to be resident Lord of your life. His words (the Scriptures) contain his commands concerning both what you are to be and what you are to do.

To accomplish this, there are two giant steps you must take. God still uses two means to establish Christ as Lord of your life: a demonstration of death and a demonstration of power.

Just as God became Lord in Egypt: You must bring the judgment of death upon your pharaoh — the "flesh," your self-centered nature.

For Christ to be Lord of your life you must face up to a cross. That is, you must be willing for God to make you as "dead" to your old selfish nature. The Holy Spirit will provide the power for you to become dead (unresponsive) to the self-centered desires of your old nature, but you must provide the *willingness*. C. S. Lewis was never more observant than in these remarks:

To surrender a self-will inflamed and swollen with years of usurpation is a kind of death. We all remember this self-will as it was in childhood, the bitter, prolonged rage at every thwarting, the burst of passionate tears, the black, satanic wish to kill or die rather than to give in.[3]

Your old nature is incorrigibly self-centered. Nothing you can do will make it obedient to God. You cannot lead the flesh into godliness. It does no good to dedicate it, educate it, motivate it, restore it, judicate it, supplicate it, militate it, alterate it, consecrate it, or attempt to transfigurate it. You must crucify it. I believe a popular term has been "you must die to self."

But some people misunderstand this. They think by "dying to self" we mean the eradication of individuality. Let this be made clear. God does not obliterate your unique personhood. It is the self-centeredness of your life that must die. God requires death to the old life of self-control, but not to the real essential you that God created and thought enough of to die for. I remember David Haney remarking, "Christ came to maximize our individuality, not minimize it." God brings your life to completion. There is a reflection of himself that he can express through your unique individuality, an image he cannot express through any other. Your mind, emotions, will, hands, eyes, feet — all have the potential for good. But there is a self-centered part of your inner nature which is thoroughly corrupt. No good thing can come from the "flesh" (Rom. 7: 18). It is this egocentric part of your nature that must die. Becoming unresponsive to your old nature is called a *crucified life!*

There is a second step toward making Christ Lord of your life. Just as God became Lord in Egypt: You must fully encounter the mighty wind of God's empowering Spirit. For Christ to actually reign as Lord of your life, you must be able to obey him as Lord. But no one can do God's bidding apart from the filling or empowering of the Holy Spirit: "And no one can (really) say, Jesus is Lord, except by and under the power and influence of the Holy Spirit" (1 Cor. 12:3). The Holy Spirit must demonstrate his power within your life before you can realize your full capacity in service.

Much of our resistance to the Holy Spirit's empowering is because of the last word in the previous sentence, service. There is considerable interest in appropriating God's power for self-benefit. But when we talk about an empowering for service to others, there are fewer takers. A choice example of this is the book entitled *I Prayed Myself Slim.* One reviewer suggested a better title might be "The Power of Positive Shrinking." The author offers the spiritual formula by which she prayed through a time of dieting and lost eighty-two pounds in ten months. Her book had one glaring deficiency.

There were about sixty prayers in the book, and only four acknowledge the existence of other people. Commenting on this in a sermon, William Sloane Coffin, Chaplain at Yale University, said: "How often we are told what God can do *for* us; how rarely what God can do *with* us".

But God stands ready to demonstrate his power within the life of any man who longs to serve Christ as Lord, as a blessing to others!

These two steps are necessary for Christ to reign as Lord of your life. The following two chapters will examine both of them. A chapter will be devoted to each.

As children we played a game called "May I?" Everyone would stand in a line except one person. He stood across from all the rest, issuing commands. He would call someone's name and say: Take four "hopping" steps, or take three "scissor" steps, or one "baby" step, or two "giant" steps. The best were those two *giant steps!*

Believe me, Christianity is no game. Yet, I would like to make an analogy. The Bible refers to self-centered Christians as babes: "For you are still only baby Christians, controlled by your own desires, not God's" (1 Cor. 3:3, TLB). Such are all those in spiritual Egypt. If this is where you are, God stands over against your life to say: "Take two giant steps." They will get you out!

As this scene ends, radiant beams of light begin to shine from the heavens down upon the stage. They are rays of hope. Israel has gained the special attention of God. "Looking down upon them, He knew that the time had come for their rescue" (Ex. 2:25, TLB).

Notes

1. William Barclay, *Jesus As They Saw Him* (New York: Harper and Row, 1963), pp. 411-412.

2. Fred H. Wight, *Highlights of Archaeology in Bible Lands* (Chicago: Moody Press, 1955), pp. 79-80.

3. C. S. Lewis, *The Problem of Pain* (New York, Macmillan Co., 1943), p. 91.

Scene 4
The First Step Out of Egypt
"The Crucified Life"

The curtain next rises on an evening scene in the land of Egypt. It is a night forever to be remembered as the night of the Passover.

The Israelite camp is strangely quiet. The streets and paths are deserted. Not one person is moving about. Every Israelite family has gathered its members inside.

Similar activity is taking place in every household. The father has brought a freshly slain lamb from their private courtyard to place it upon a burning altar. The lamb was especially chosen, without spot or blemish. Blood from the lamb has been placed on two side posts and the upper post of their leather-hinged front door.

The family members are gathered within a second, inner room which was so characteristic of their dwellings. They are seated around a table upon which rests a single homemade clay lamp. The family is preparing to eat the roasted flesh of the lamb, with unleavened bread and bitter herbs, symbolizing their years of slavery.

Soon the silence of their camp will be broken. A mournful cry from every Egyptian home in Goshen will rise and spread across the plain, echoing through the deserted streets of the Israelite camp. A judgment of death has been passed upon Egypt, because Pharaoh would not let God's children go. God's death angel is about to pass over the land. The first born of every household will die. But the Israelite homes will be spared. Because the blood of a sacrificial lamb is upon their doors, God's judgment will *pass over* them. The Passover!

"When I see the blood, I will pass over you" (Ex. 12:13).

You are witness to the Passover, as recorded in the twelfth
chapter of Exodus. And the Passover, then, was a judgment of
death passed upon Pharaoh, for the deliverance of Israel from
Egypt!

Several years ago I wrote two words above the twelfth chapter of Exodus in my Bible: *The Cross.* It was the first time I
consciously recall reading that particular chapter, but I was
immediately impressed how well it typified the crucifixion. It
revealed Calvary to me as clearly as if a cross had been lightly
preprinted across the page and the passage printed over it.
The cross seemed to underlie all that was said in the chapter.
For the cross was God's judgment upon the sins of our flesh (our
Pharaoh), and is our means of deliverance from sin (Egypt).

The sacrifice of the lamb is a foretype of Christ, the lamb of
God, who "gave himself to God for our sins as one sacrifice for
all time" (Heb. 10:12, TLB). Just as the Israelites shed the
blood of a special lamb, one without spot or blemish, you are
redeemed "with the precious blood of Christ, as a lamb without
blemish and without spot" (1 Pet. 1:19). That the Passover
points to the crucifixion is unquestionable. First Corinthians
makes a direct application of it: "For even Christ our passover
is sacrificed for us" (1 Cor. 5:7).

Jesus died to deliver us from the penalty and the practice
of sin. When God told Israel to commemorate the Passover
night with an annual celebration, they were to recall their
deliverance: "And it shall come to pass, when your children
shall say unto you, What mean ye by this service? That ye
shall say, It is the sacrifice of the Lord's passover, who passed
over the houses of the children of Israel in Egypt, when he
smote the Egyptians, and *delivered* our houses" (Ex. 12:26-27,
italics added).

It is so until this day. Modern Jews keep Yom Kippur as their
day of atonement. On this day they celebrate their forgiveness.
On this day devout Jews think of their sins, repent, and ask
forgiveness. But they also celebrate Passover in memory of
their deliverance. Passover is celebrated in memory of the
freeing of the Jews from slavery in Egypt.

Moreover, when Paul made reference to the Passover in chapter 5 of 1 Corinthians, the emphasis was on deliverance from the practice of sin! The chapter speaks of judging sin (v. 3) and putting it away from you (v. 13). Referring to the unleavened bread used in the Passover, this application is made: "Know ye not that a little leaven leaveneth the whole lump? Purge out therefore the old leaven, that ye may be a new lump, as ye are unleavened. For even Christ our passover is sacrificed for us" (1 Cor. 5:6-7).

The deliverance of the children of Israel from Egypt symbolizes deliverance from the bondage of an old nature. You must "purge out the old leaven, that ye may be a new lump." That is, purge out the old nature that your entire life might be spiritually renewed.

You will never establish Christ as Lord of your life without "purging out" (deliverance from) the old nature. And your old nature was put to death on Calvary's cross: "your old sin-loving nature 'died' with Christ" (Rom. 6:8, TLB). But you must believe it is so and count it as so by faith for this death to become a reality within your daily experience of life. An explanation of how this is done will conclude this chapter, but first be convinced that the way of spiritual victory is the principle of life through death!

Life Through Death Is the Way of Natural Life

In the southernmost tip of Texas there is a beautiful and productive delta region called "The Valley." The area is renowned for its fruitful citrus groves.

While in a crusade there, I learned something about orange trees that fascinated me. The sweet orange seedling cannot grow in The Valley. Growers must first plant a sturdy "root stock," which is a stronger type of orange tree. But this root-stock tree produces a bitter fruit. Therefore, after the root stock takes hold and becomes a young tree, they graft in a different natured orange — the sweet orange tree which produces marketable fruit.

This is how it is done. A cross is cut into the bark of the old root-stock tree. Then the bud of a sweet-natured orange is grafted into it through that crosscut. Once embedded there, it is allowed to grow until there is evidence of life.

However, all you really have at this point is a two-natured tree. If nothing else is done to the old root stock, the new-natured bud would produce nothing more than a spindly limb. Depending on how much life-sap the old root-stock would allow it, the new orange limb would grow for a while but eventually retard. Lacking the strength to hold itself up, it would grow out, then bend down, and lie out along the ground. It would make a deformed bush of itself but would never become a sweet orange tree as it was meant to be.

The old root stock would grow on and produce its bitter fruit. The sweet orange limb would draw enough sap to sustain its life but would never bear fruit!

Therefore, after the sweet orange has been grafted in, the fruit growers wait until there is evidence of life. Then, just above the graft, they cut off the old root stock! Once the old root stock has been cut off, the full sap supply flows into the sweet orange limb. At this point, with the added help of an outside stake the young limb will begin to grow upward.

After a time the stake may be removed. The sweet orange limb will become a tree. The entire tree trunk will straighten, and become a fruit-producing orange tree growing out of an old root stock.

But always remember, though the root stock has been cut off, the old sour orange roots remain and will continually try to put out new sour orange limbs. These limbs inevitably manifest themselves below the graft. They are called suckers.

These suckers must be constantly cut off or there will be a desperate struggle within the tree and these root-stock limbs will take over. The suckers will recapture the life sap supply. They will gain dominance and will eventually produce their bitter fruit. The sweet orange nature will wither back and become fruitless unless the suckers are constantly pruned!

Life Through Death Is the Way of Spiritual Life

Conversely, there is a parallel between the sweet orange seedling and spiritual life. As the seedling needs the sour orange root stock, the Holy Spirit needs a body through which to express the nature of Christ in our world.

Your body is the root stock God has chosen. But your flesh nature produces only bitter fruit: "Adultery, fornication, uncleanness, lasciviousness, idolatry, witchcraft, hatred, variance, emulations, wrath, strife, seditions, heresies, envyings, murders, drunkenness" (Gal. 5:19-21).

However, when you become a Christian through Calvary's cross, the Lord's nature is grafted into your life: "And have put on the new nature, which is being constantly renewed in the image of its Creator" (Col. 3:10, NEB).[1] Though you receive a new nature, you retain your old one (as discussed in chapter 1) and if nothing is done with that old nature, your new nature will grow very little.

The old nature must now be "cut off." If not, like the old root stock, it will go on producing its bitter fruit. And your new nature will resemble the retarded sweet orange limb which grows, then bends down, and lies out along the ground like a deformed, fruitless bush. Your spiritual life will never bear fruit.

But with your old nature "cut off," the Holy Spirit can make a brand-new person out of you, created in the likeness of him: "Put off . . . the old man, which is corrupt according to the deceitful lusts; and be renewed in the spirit of your mind; and that ye put on the new man, which after God is created in righteousness and true holiness" (Eph. 4:22-24).

Be assured you will never know his lordship to the fullest apart from death to your old flesh nature. Your "flesh" is your "Pharaoh." Your flesh (old nature) will retain control of your life as stubbornly as Pharaoh retained his grasp on Israel. You must render a judgment of death upon the flesh. This is called a *crucified life!*

This Is the Way to Victory

What, then, truly frees you to obey the Lord — with all of your life? I want to list the steps very carefully.

(1) Be aware of your "old nature" — the self-centered bent of your life. Recognize it for what it is: the source of all your sin.

(2) Render a judgment of death. Realizing no spiritual good can ever come from your old self-centered nature (Rom. 7:18), you must pass a sentence of death upon it. You must write out your own obituary and die! . . . "And they that are Christ's, have crucified the flesh with the affections and lusts" (Gal. 5:24).

(3) Believe God will deaden you to every selfish act and attitude of your fleshly nature (Eph. 2:3-10). Furthermore, God has already put you to death, potentially, to your old nature. "Your old evil desires were nailed to the cross with him; that part of you that loves to sin was crushed and fatally wounded . . . your sin-loving nature 'died' with Christ" (Rom. 6:6,8, TLB). That same judgment, which has been rendered by the high court of heaven and executed at Calvary, now must be carried out in your experience to become a reality in your life! God will accomplish this by the power of His Spirit (Rom. 8:13). You are to ask the Holy Spirit to do it, believing he will! Actually pray and verbally count yourself as dead to everything that might alienate your affection from God, then ask the Holy Spirit to make it so.

(4) Be complete with it. To be certain you do not keep a selfish grasp on anything, be sure to release everything. Place every minute detail of your life on the cross, one thing at a time. You do this by telling God of your willingness to become as unresponsive as he would have you to be to: your job, your future, your wife or sweetheart, your golf clubs, your fishing gear, your wardrobe, your friends, your home, your family, your tool box, your books, your television, your meals, your hobbies, your pocketbook, your abilities, your social activities, your responsibilities, your reputation, your most

treasured possessions, your fears, your worries, your guilts, your accomplishments, your failures, your temperament, your habits, your schedule, your likes and dislikes, your conduct and your character, every act and attitude, and all your material possessions.

Be honest with God and yourself. Place them in the grave one by one, saying: "Lord, I don't want these in my life. I die to this and to that." Believe the Holy Spirit for strength to offer up all your life, even as Jesus did, "Who through the eternal Spirit offered himself without spot to God" (Heb. 9:14). The disciples "forsook all, and followed him" (Luke 5:11). He will expect no less of you!

(5) Resurrect only those things which clear conviction will assure you are a part of God's plan for your life.

(6) Now ask the Holy Spirit to make Christ Lord of your life (1 Cor. 12:3; Rom. 8:11).

Think with me about this point. One day you hauled down the old flag of self-enthronement and raised the white flag of surrender. You received Christ to be Lord of your life. Wonderful!

Now you must follow through with your decision. Begin allowing Christ to *become* the Lord you have received him to *be!* To confess Christ as Lord is one thing; to possess him as Lord is another. Now take positive action. Give him the master key into the every area of your life. Let him adjust your entire schedule to fit his plans for you. Depend on his strength for every task. Learn to shift the weight of life upon him and let him carry the heavy end of every burden. Grant him full authority over all your activities and consult him in everything. Take Christ into your daily routine of living and introduce him as Lord of every situation!

At the conclusion of a meeting a lady asked to speak with me. "I must share my victory," she said. "There was *one* area of my life where I have refused to let Christ be Lord. I have balked at this for years.

"You see," she continued, "my husband and I go down to

Dallas in the winter, and to be a part of the people down there I became a collector."

"Pardon," I replied.

"A collector," she repeated. "Down there people collect things for a hobby, so I decided to start me a collection. I chose bottles. And you see, inevitably the most beautiful bottles are wine, beer, and whiskey bottles. Now I do not drink, but for years I have realized many did not know this. Because every time someone enters our home, all over our shelves are wine and whiskey bottles. And, somehow, a rebellion had formed in my heart. It seemed my self-centeredness manifested itself in this one thing. Deep within I knew that this collection was something I would not give up even if God wanted me to, and sometimes I have the strangest feeling he did want me to.

"There were times I felt all those whiskey bottles did little to enhance our Christian witness. But this was a 'festering point' in my life. I was going to do what I wanted at this point. That is, until I finally came to the place in my life when I was ready to die to self. Last Tuesday I sat down and wrote out my obituary. Then I arose and gathered every bottle in my home, and carried them out on the back porch. I took a hammer, and I broke every single bottle to pieces. My neighbor came running over, I guess she thought I had lost my mind. But with every blow of the hammer, I could feel myself being set free, as if shackles were dropping to the ground. Several times that evening I returned to my back porch and just stood for a while, towering over the broken pieces of my former rebellion. I have never felt so liberated in all my life! Life has never been so thrilling. I know I am wholly his, and this confidence has filled my life with peace and confidence like I have never known. Each day it gets better. I have learned the real meaning of those words: 'Free at last, free at last, thank God almighty, free at last!' "

As the curtain closes on this scene, the light of day begins to appear above the eastern horizon. The night of the Passover has ended. The *day* of their passing over has begun: "That very day the Lord brought out the people of Israel from the land of Egypt, wave after wave of them crossing the border" (Ex. 12:51, TLB).

The first step out of Egypt is a crucified life!

If you have never really been dead to self, I suggest you get alone with God, kneel with this book open before you, and prayerfully do everything suggested in the six steps of this chapter. Then, turn to the Traveler's Aids in the back of this book; read the first one at the top of the page. Fill out your Obituary Notice. Follow the instructions for Daily Self-Destruction! This will keep you free!

Notes

1. Scripture quotations marked "NEB" are from The New English Bible, Old Testament © The Delegates of the Oxford University Press, and the Syndics of the Cambridge University Press, 1970, and The New English Bible, New Testament, © The Delegates of the Oxford University Press, and the Syndics of the Cambridge University Press, 1961. Reprinted by permission.

Scene 5
The Second Step
Out of Egypt
"The Spirit-Filled Life"

As the curtain rises, the spotlight is fixed upon the stalwart figure of Moses. The waters of the Red Sea are behind him and a group of distinguished looking men are seated before him. They have gathered at the seashore for what is obviously a high-level conference.

They have arrived with scowling faces. And the reason for their concern is obvious. In the distance you can see the encircled campfires of several thousand soldiers. Pharaoh had again turned on Israel. His army had finally overtaken them, had encamped, and intended to recapture them on the next morning. Israel's position was perilous. The Red Sea was before them, Pharaoh's regiments had approached from behind, then fanned out to trap them on the shoreline.

But Moses has a word from heaven. God is about to demonstrate his power. A hush falls over the assembled leaders as Moses stands to speak. His words fall like thunderbolts as he rebukes them for their fear. Suddenly, Moses raises his rod and a forceful east wind arrives and sweeps the pillar of clouds over between the Egyptians and the Israelites. As the clouds begin to stack up, twilight is changed to a prenatural darkness above the Egyptians, and envelopes them. As Moses keeps his rod held high, the moonlight reflects off the pillar of clouds so that there is light enough in Israel's camp for them to pack-up and march. Moses then commands the Israelites to arise and go forward. As he does, Moses turns and sweeps the rod of God out over the Red Sea. Immediately the east wind increases with multiplied intensity. The wind veritably blasts a path across the Red Sea, drying the ground and stacking up the waters like a wall.

All through the night the wind continues to hold the water back, as the children of Israel make their way across on dry land. By early dawn the Egyptian armies discover what has happened and follow the children of Israel in hot pursuit. Following along the line of the Israelite retreat, the Egyptians find the channel still dry, and hastily enter it with their chariot force. But the instant Israel's rearguard reaches the far bank, the winds cease, and the waters reconverge to drown Pharaoh's forces in the sea.

A deafening roar of victory echoes across the valley. The children of Israel are beside themselves, leaping for joy and embracing each other. But just as quickly silence falls, as some children call their attention again to the sea. A ghastly mass of Egyptian corpses are thrown up by the tide on the Asiatic shore. The demonstration of God's power has a thrilling yet sobering effect, it is an awesome sight.

But you need such demonstration of power. Because it is one thing to get out of Egypt. It is another thing to stay out. A *crucified life* brings you out of the self-centered enslavement of spiritual Egypt, but it takes something else to keep you out. This is a perilous stage in your spiritual development! Let me explain.

God changed your life from within. Therefore, to gain victory in your life, it was imperative to turn your attention inward. You needed to see that old nature as "rotten through and through" (Rom. 7:18, TLB). You needed the hope of your inward nature being renewed in his likeness. You needed to be sure of his lordship within.

Yet, there is a danger with this. Time and again, I have watched Christians experience great spiritual victory within their "inner lives," only to become "spiritually introverted." Having tasted the sweet joys of inward renewal, they turn all their attention within themselves. They get involved in endless study groups to learn more about the "inner man." They chase around from conference to conference simply to learn some

new truth about themselves. They shut themselves in to read
book after book — while the world goes to hell! Please
understand, there is nothing wrong with study groups and con-
ferences — if they are oriented to redemptive action!

I know of some pastors in strategic churches who have been
"turned off" from much emphasis on the deeper spiritual life.
They have seen so many who supposedly have experienced
great personal victory, yet do little to share Christ with others.

It is an amazing phenomenon! You can actually be liberated from a selfish inner nature, only to become so infatuated
with the exhilarating enjoyment of self-discovery and self-improvement that your life resumes its self-centered hub! Ignor-
ing the needs of others, you become preoccupied with your own
condition — a compulsive spiritual "pulse-taker." Your life
gets so heavy with self-concern you "high center" on selfishness! Without realizing it, your life is self-centered again, and
you are enslaved anew!

You are never safely out of spiritual Egypt until you cross
a line (Red Sea) where you cease to think of yourself and begin to serve in the power of God as a witness to others of him!

God brought Israel out of Egypt to serve him, not to be re-
enslaved in service to Pharaoh. The Bible mentions this often:
"Let my people go, that they may serve me" (Ex. 8:20).
"Let my people go, that they may serve me" (Ex. 9:1).
"Let my people go, that they may serve me" (Ex. 9:13).
"Let my people go, that they may serve me" (Ex. 10:3).

Furthermore, the one objective of all their service was a wit-
ness to others: "And the Egyptians shall know that I am the
Lord" (Ex. 14:18). God demonstrated his power at the Red
Sea as a witness through the Israelites to the Egyptians.

God has the power to see you through the wilderness to a
spiritual promised land of abundance. But this power is only
available for those who serve, as a witness of him!

God will give you a Red Sea experience. Just as he de-
ployed his mighty power to lead Israel out into service, as a
witness of him, God will also express his power in you, as you
go out in service, to witness of him. Your Red Sea experience

is called the "filling of the Spirit." You need it to journey on. Let me explain.

The Explanation of a Spirit-Filled Life

Just what is it to be "filled" with the Spirit? Well, contrary to what you might expect, to be "filled" is not to receive more of the Spirit. Rather, the Spirit gets more of you!

Three times the New Testament makes a comparison between the effect of drinking wine and the effect of being filled with the Spirit. It was said of John the Baptist: "He . . . shall drink neither wine nor strong drink; and he shall be filled with the Holy Ghost" (Luke 1:15). On the day of Pentecost someone commented: "These men are full of new wine." But the Bible states they were "filled with Holy Spirit" (Acts 2:4,13). Finally, Paul said: "And be not drunk with wine, wherein is excess; but be filled with the Spirit" (Eph. 5:18).

When one is "drunk with wine," it is not that he consumes enough to fill his body with liquid like filling a bottle — from the top of his head to the tip of his toe. He is overcome by the wine, intoxicated. Similarly, when one is "filled with the Spirit," it is not that he receives so much of the Spirit that he fills up inside from his head to his heels. But he is overcome by the Spirit! To be filled, then, is not to receive more of the Spirit. But the Spirit receives more of you!

You receive as much of the Spirit as you will ever need, the moment you are saved. But at your invitation, he will take a stronger grip on your life to use it effectively in his service. You are "full" of the Spirit when it is God, not you, accomplishing the task. Things will happen that it takes God to explain! Thus your life is not a witness to your efforts, but to his. Apply this test: If you can explain the effectiveness of all your service in terms of your energies and abilities, you are not serving in the fullness of the Spirit!

It is in this sense Gerald Kennedy says, "The Holy Spirit is essentially an experience."[1] The filling of the Spirit is an experience by which God acts in human life. To be filled is to be empowered, to be overcome by God, so that he might accomplish his work through you.

You are filled with power. And the dictionary defines "power" as force or energy applied to work. You are filled for service. You can be filled for one task. You can also be filled continuously if your life-style is geared to redemptive action!

The "filling of the Spirit" is the empowering of your life in service for his witness through you to others. It seems to me there are several clarifications that beg for expression at this point. I will state them affirmatively. From what the Bible actually teaches, the "filling of the Spirit" is not so much for the reproduction of his life *in* you as it is for the expression of his life *through* you. Think about it! Correspondingly, you are not filled with power to exercise a gift, so much as to express the giver!

There comes a time for every truly committed Christian, when to journey on requires you to be filled with the power of God. If you are one who has died to your old self-centered nature, the time to be "filled," for you, is now!

Having invited the Lord to come and live his life in you, choose death to your old selfish nature and seek the expression of his life through you to others. As you enter a life-style of service with an objective of witnessing, the Holy Spirit will fill you with power!

The Evidence of a Spirit-Filled Life

The evidence of a Spirit-filled life is power! In essence, the Spirit-filled life is a Spirit-empowered life. The power of a Spirit-filled life will manifest itself in two ways. First, it will be overwhelming in its experience. The Greek word which the authorized New Testament translates "filled," is the word *Pletho*. It could well be translated by the word "overcome." It is often used to convey this meaning in the New Testament:

In Luke 5:7, the ships were filled (overcome) and began to sink.

In Luke 6:11, they were filled (overcome) with madness.

In Acts 3:10, they were filled (overcome) with wonder.
In Acts 5:17, they were filled (overcome) with indignation.
In Acts 13:45, they were filled (overcome) with envy.
In Acts 19:29, they were filled (overcome) with confusion.

To be filled is to be overcome! It follows then, to be filled with the Spirit is to be overcome by the Spirit, so that he takes over, to multiply the effectiveness of your witness. Samuel Shoemaker says that true spiritual power of the Christian order is a kind of possessedness.

There are many conflicting ideas concerning what takes place when you are "filled with the Spirit." I have spent hours upon hours examining contrasting views on what the "filling" is. Finally, it dawned upon me that we have one viewpoint that is divinely inspired. Luke provides the only authentic account of what happened when New Testament Christians were filled with the Spirit. He recorded many such experiences in the book of Acts. A careful examination of each account will reveal the first Christians were "overcome" by a power beyond themselves, which enabled them to serve as powerful witnesses of Christ. The initial promise was: "Ye shall receive power . . . and ye shall be witnesses unto me" (Acts 1:8). That is precisely what happened. "And they were all filled with the Holy Ghost, and began to speak with other tongues [in foreign language, Acts 2:6,11] as the Spirit gave them utterance" (Acts 2:4).

In numerous passages, Luke records similar experiences:

"Then Peter filled with the Holy Ghost, said . . . now when they saw the boldness of Peter . . . they marveled" (Acts 4:8, 13).

"And they were all filled with the Holy Ghost, and spoke the word of God with boldness . . . and with great power gave the apostles witness" (Acts 4:31,33).

"And they chose Stephen, a man full of faith and of the Holy Ghost. And Stephen, full of faith and power, did great wonders and miracles among the people" (Acts 6:5,8).

Also of Stephen, Acts records; "he, being of the Holy Ghost" spoke with such convincing power that his listeners were "cut to the heart" (Acts 7:54,55).

"And they received the Holy Ghost . . . and when Simon saw . . . the Holy Ghost was given [Notice: it was obvious] he offered them money, saying give me also this power" (Acts 8:17-19).

Paul was "filled with the Holy Ghost . . . and straightway he preached Christ in the synagogues . . . all that heard him were amazed" (Acts 9:17,20,21).

Peter verifies that "God anointed Jesus of Nazareth with the Holy Ghost and with power: who went about doing good" (Acts 10:38).

"On the Gentiles also was poured out the gift of the Holy Ghost, for they heard them speak with tongues and magnify God" (Acts 10:45).

"Then Saul . . . filled with the Holy Ghost," preached with power and "the deputy, when he saw what was done, believed, being astonished at the doctrine of the Lord" (Acts 13:9,12).

"The Holy Ghost came on them; and they spoke with tongues, and prophesied" (Acts 19:6).

I have listed every eyewitness account of someone being filled with the Spirit. Forgetting all preconceived ideas, this is what actually happened. Each recorded account bears these similarities: (1) Those "filled" were visibly overcome with power. (2) Their "filling" is mentioned in direct connection with their service. (3) In most cases their service was a *witness* by vocal expression.

This brings us back to my previous statement. When the first Christians were filled, they were overcome by a power beyond themselves, which enabled them to serve as powerful witnesses of Christ.

Griffith Thomas recognized a similar experience in the life of Christ, as the Lord began his ministry: "When the Holy Spirit came upon Christ at his baptism, it was initiation into, and consecration to specific service for God . . . and with this came an adequate bestowal of power."[2]

What a stupendous encouragement! When we commit our lives to a consistent life-style of witness to others, we can ap-

propriate a fullness of power for the expression of that witness!
It will be overwhelming in its experience.

There is a second characteristic of a Spirit-empowered life.
It is irresistible in its effect.

An interesting thing about these examples of a Spirit-filled
witness, as recorded in Acts: there was obvious response
from those who heard it. They were "confounded" (Acts
2:6). They "marvelled" (Acts 4:13). They "cried out" (Acts
7:57). They were "amazed" (Acts 9:21). They were "astonished" (Acts 10:45; 13:12).

In each case their Spirit-empowered witness was irresistible.
There was always a response. No one ignored them. There
was always a reaction. Sometimes people responded positively.
Three thousand were saved in response to Peter's witness at
Pentecost (Acts 2:41). At other times people responded
negatively. In reaction to Stephen's Spirit-filled witness, they
cried out with a loud voice, placed hands on their ears, and
ran at him. They cast him out of the city and stoned him (Acts
7:57-58).

But no one was impassive to their witness. The Spirit-filled
witness is irresistible in its effect. There is always a response,
either positive or negative! But something happens!

Someone has said, "God's biddings are enablings." God
will never call you to a service without providing a witness of
himself through that service — in his power. Every demand
upon your life is a demand upon the Spirit within you. There is
power available for all God wants done in this world. Just
plug in and turn on!

Richard Hogue is an evangelist who preaches with a heavenly enduement of power. One night three thousand people
responded to his preaching, to accept Christ as Lord and Savior of their life. Last year God wrought an average of well
over one hundred decisions for Christ every night Richard
Hogue preached. But every real man of God has known this
anointing of power to some degree. Millions would give testimony of a unique power upon their lives in Christian service.

This power, to the degree you need it, is available to all who witness of Christ.

Your witness can reach out and grab someone like a "grappling hook." When a "grappling hook" takes hold, it tears the flesh to pull away. The object must allow itself to be pulled in. Likewise, there is persuasive power in a Spirit-filled witness. Those who refuse might even compensate for the convicting pain you have caused them and vocally lash out at you. Others will be brought to the Lord. But no one is likely to ignore you!

Yes, the evidence of a Spirit-filled life is power: overwhelming in its experience and irresistible in its effect. A. Leonard Griffith has well said: "If the New Testament makes one thing clear, it is this: the identifying mark of the church is not doctrinal, liturgical, or ecclesiastical correctness, but the presence and power of the Holy Spirit."[3]

The Entrance into a Spirit-Filled Life

How does one come to be filled with Spirit? That is the question of real consequence.

The Scriptures speak of five requirements for being filled with the Holy Spirit. These same principles naturally carry over with regard to receiving the fullness of the Spirit.

(1) *You come thirsting.* Jesus established this simple prerequisite when he arose in the temple to say:

"If anyone is thirsty, let him come to me; whoever believes in me, let him drink." As Scripture says, "Streams of living water shall flow out from within him." He was speaking of the Spirit which believers in him would receive later (John 7:37-39; NEB).

A certain amount of desire is necessary in order to be Spirit-filled. Nothing is promised to the casual "window-shopper." God measures your readiness by the intensity of your desire!

(2) *You come confessing.* Peter spoke of the necessity of repentance for receiving the Holy Spirit: "Then Peter said unto them, Repent . . . and ye shall receive the gift of the Holy Spirit" (Acts 2:38).

A man can no more be filled with the Spirit and full of sin at the same time than a vessel can be filled with both light and darkness. They are mutually exclusive!

The filling of the Spirit awaits your willingness to deal with sin in your life. Repent of your sin. To repent is to thoroughly deal with it. Confess it. Acknowledge it. Name it. Admit it. Forsake it. Ask to be forgiven. Then claim your cleansing: "If we confess our sins, he is faithful and just to forgive us our sins, and to cleanse us from all unrighteousness" (1 John 1:9).

(3) *You come obeying.* The early Christians did not receive the Holy Spirit simply because an apostle laid hands upon them. God required their obedience: "And we are his witnesses of these things; and so is also the Holy Ghost, whom God hath given to them that *obey* him" (Acts 5:32, italics added).

When you come to be filled with the Spirit, it is like a servant reporting for duty. The "filling" is an empowering. God empowers your service for a witness of himself. God knows your intent. If you are spiritually "unemployed," you won't need to be filled with power. You won't use it! God won't waste it! You won't get it! Many are the persons who have prayed to be filled and experienced nothing, because they did not seek power for service. They sought prestige for self-glory. Some wanted a talent for service more than triumph in service. Some wanted an exhibition of their gift more than an expression of their God.

Pray to be filled with his Spirit, then depart to serve. The filling comes only as you go, and to the degree that you go! As you go, obey every impulse of your day and do what he wishes. You will experience the filling as he empowers your service — for a witness of himself. You will experience that "something other than you" — an effectiveness which only comes from Christ.

In summer crusades, our evangelistic team holds classes for teens during the day. On the day we lead them to seek a filling of the Spirit, we then send them out to blitz their city, witnessing to everyone they meet. They return breathlessly, telling of an overcoming power. They speak of a new boldness in witnessing, a new authority, persuasive power, and telling effect! They see things happen which can only be explained in terms of the Holy Spirit. They discover the thrill of being used of God. They go home to share with parents this new-found joy in serving Jesus.

You can be filled if you want to serve in power!

(4) *You came asking.* Jesus promised the Spirit to those who ask: "If ye then, being evil, know how to give good gifts unto your children: how much more shall your heavenly Father give the Holy Spirit to them that ask him" (Luke 11:13)? Therefore, when the disciples later sought the Spirit's fullness, they simply asked in prayer: "And when they had prayed . . . they were all filled with the Holy Ghost" (Acts 4:31). "Who, when they were come down, prayed for them, that they might receive the Holy Ghost . . . and they received the Holy Ghost" (Acts 8:15,17).

But keep this in mind: the filling of the Spirit is not a luxury for which you beg and plead. To the contrary, God commands you to be filled! The grammatical construction of the sentence reveals it was in the imperative mood in which a military command was given, that Paul stated in Ephesians: "Be filled with the Spirit" (Eph. 5:18).

God has commanded you to be filled — just ask!

(5) *You come believing.* The only other biblical prerequisite for receiving the Holy Spirit is faith: "That we might receive the promise of the Spirit through faith" (Gal. 3:14). However, this is *not* the least difficult. It is my personal conviction that many have asked for the Spirit's fullness in futility because they lacked faith to believe God would, indeed, fill them. They have asked, and asked, and asked. Now they need to stop asking and start trusting.

James S. McConkey is quite correct in stressing that nothing is more hurtful than to ask for the fullness of his Spirit and then constantly inspect our lives to see if God is fulfilling his promise.[4] That's like a child who constantly digs up the seed

to see if it has sprouted. All that introspection is a subtle unbelief, a fear that perhaps God will not be faithful to fulfill
his promise. Back of all this is also a greater desire for the
blessing than for the blessor. Bonhoeffer opts for "hidden
righteousness," based on faith God will do what he promises
to do!

Let us concern ourselves with the conditions of fullness, not
the manifestation. Meet God's condition, then ask, and depart
to serve, believing you are filled!

No one is a final authority in matters of the Holy Spirit. We
are all only reporters. For whatever it may be worth, I have
but shared the way in which I appropriate his fullness in my
own life.

First, I test the intensity of my thirst: Am I praying
mechanically or with fresh, heartfelt desire? (I come thirsting.)

Next, I ask God to reveal each sin he wishes me to confess,
and then I claim forgiveness of my sins. (I come confessing.)

Then I reckon myself dead to self-centeredness. I yield myself, asking the Spirit to quicken me to obedience in everything
the Lord would have me do. I report for duty and depart to
serve, trusting his empowering for all I do. (I come obeying.)

Regardless of the cost, I ask to be filled. (I come asking.)

Lastly, I simply claim his fullness. I thank him for filling
me. (I come believing.)

What I have just said has reference to daily filling. I begin
every day praying in just this manner. However, the first time
you seek the fullness of God's Spirit, special stress should be
placed on the first two steps: thirsting and confessing.

It must be emphasized that your initial experience of being
filled should center around a time of serious and honest confession. I suggest you set aside an hour. Begin by reading
Psalm 139:23-24 and Jeremiah 17:9-10. Ask God to lead you
in searching your life for all unconfessed sin. Turn to the sin-
list at the end of chapter 7. It should stimulate an awareness
of the sin that needs to be confessed, perhaps in your own life.

At this point, follow missionary Bertha Smith's suggestion
and take a clean sheet of paper. Write out each and every

sin God brings to your mind. Then confess those sins to God. Next, go back through your list and mark out some of your sins — the ones between you and God alone.

There will be other sins against your fellowman and God. Review these. Beside each, write out the action you will take to make restitution. You can never be right with God unless you are right with your fellowman. A young boy in California took back over a hundred dollars' worth of stolen items to a sporting goods store. Begin by getting right with every fellow church member with whom you have an unsettled disagreement. One employer called all his employees into the office and confessed his inconsistency, announcing a policy of Christian ethics which would prevail in all business transactions from that day forward. There are those I've known who have confessed harbored resentments, their lethargy in positions of church leadership, and negative attitudes. One lady went back to her home church and apologized before the entire congregation for critical remarks she had made. Many have had to ask forgiveness of those they have slandered. Many have had to pay bad debts. A friend of mine returned two books he had borrowed from me but had failed to return — which convicted me and I returned one of his. One minister wrote an apology to a seminary professor for cheating in his class. Young people have asked forgiveness from their parents. One man sat down and wrote out a check to repay ten thousand dollars he had borrowed but failed to repay some twenty years before. He also paid interest on each year at the going rate — a considerable sum!

Keep one thing in mind. A spiritual principle should be followed only to the extent it does not cross another one. For example, one should never publicly confess a sin that would harm another. Never cleanse your conscience with someone else's tears.

Having vowed to make restitution for all these sins, cross out the entire page and claim God's forgiveness! Then you are ready to be filled with the Spirit. But follow through by obeying, asking, and believing.

One last word concerning thirsting. Paul S. Rees tells of a Keswick Conference in which a preacher enumerated the great blessings which came in his ministry as a consequence of Spirit-filled service. Following the sermon, a young man came to the speaker and said, "I am so thirsty. I need the power of the Spirit in my life."

The preacher said, "I can take you to the place where I was filled, and anyone can be filled at that place. Would you like to come with me?"

"Yes, by all means," the young man replied.

So they walked out of the conference grounds and up a mountain. As they sauntered along, the preacher kept talking about the glory resulting from a Spirit-filled life. Once in a while the young man would come to a clearing in the woods and ask, "Is this the place?"

"No, but it isn't much farther; it's up here a little distance."

They kept walking. The preacher kept talking. The young man's thirst kept increasing.

They reached a plateau and the young man asked again, "Is this the place?"

He asked the same when they walked out into a valley, again at the edge of a clearing, and at the top of each hill.

"Is this the place?" he asked again and again. Finally, he could stand it no longer. He fell upon his knees and all but shouted, "I can't go any farther. I must pray to be filled right now!"

The preacher turned and said: *"This is the place! This is the place!"*

Do you see? When you come to the place where you want to be filled with the Spirit more than anything else in the world, that's the place where you will be filled!

When you are filled, God will miraculously bring you through to victories in service as surely as he brought Israel through the Red Sea.

As the curtain falls, the waters of the Red Sea roll between Israel and Egypt, and the children of Israel break forth in a magnificent song of triumph: "Thy right hand, O Lord, is become glorious in power . . . for the horses of Pharaoh went in with his chariots and with his horsemen into the sea, and the Lord brought again the waters of the sea upon them; but the children of Israel went on dry land in the midst of the sea" (Ex. 15:6, 19) and thousands of voices ring the curtain down!

You can be filled right now! Turn back to the Travelers Aids and read the one for the Spirit at the middle of that page. That contains your daily filling instructions. Use them constantly!

Notes

1. Gerald Kennedy, *Have This Mind,* (New York: Harper and Brothers), p. 44.

2. W. Griffith Thomas, *The Holy Spirit of God* (Grand Rapids: Wm. B. Eerdmans Publishing Co., 1963), p. 42.

3. A. Leonard Griffith, *God and His People* (Nashville: Abingdon Press, 1961), p. 57.

4. James S. McConkey, *Three-Fold Secret of the Holy Spirit* (Chicago: Moody Press).

ACT 2
Wilderness
Wanderings

Scene 6
What the Wilderness Is
"God's Testing Ground"

The curtain opens as morning breaks across the vast camp of Israel. The Israelites are camped in a meadow near the Red Sea shoreline. At the center of the camp, camels are kneeling in circles, while drivers are busy with final adjustments of saddlebags, girths, and water bottles. The tents have long been folded and packed. Children are running on last-minute errands.

The signal is finally given by Moses and the shrill notes of a ram's horn pierce the sky. Beginning with the eastern tribe, group after group peel away from the camp, soon forming a vast caravan. The camels move off with their heads held high, their bodies in smooth but endless motion, and their soft feet shuffling over the ground.

The wilderness is a wild place, stony, hard, with ragged rocks

and cruel reddish hills which blaze in the sunlight like hot
tarnished bronze. Beyond the rugged hills lies the desert, like
an interminable yellow emptiness.

One question fills the mind of every Israelite as they set
forth this day: Why the wilderness? Had not God promised
them the land of Canaan? But the land of Canaan was
Northeast, and their caravan is headed almost due South!
Furthermore, there is a short trade route through the Philistine
territory that makes the Promised Land relatively near. But
this is just the point: when God led the children of Israel out
of Egypt, he did not lead them into the Promised Land immediately: "And it came to pass, when Pharaoh had let the
people go, that God led them not through the way of the land
of the Philistines [the Promised Land] *although that* was near.
. . . But God led the people about, through the way of the
wilderness of the Red Sea (Ex. 13:17-18, italics added).

Think about it! The Promised Land was near. But God led
the people about, through the wilderness. Why the detour?
The Bible says, "God led the people about, through the way
of the wilderness." God was directing them!

You see, God led them through the wilderness because they
weren't ready for the warfare! He stated such: "God led them
not through the way of the land of the Philistines [Promised
Land], although that was near; for God said, *lest peradventure
the people repent when they see war, and they return to Egypt"*
(Ex. 13:17, italics added).

The Promised Land was enemy-occupied territory. There
would be no taking it without a battle. Therefore, God did not
lead the Israelites into the Promised Land immediately upon
their release from Egypt. They were not prepared for combat.
They might have deserted and returned to Egypt! To enter
Canaan was to engage in warfare, and war must be prepared
for.

It is the same in your spiritual journey. God will not lead
you out of spiritual Egypt and immediately into the Promised
Land. You are not ready for the warfare! Satan mounts his
most devastating attack against you in the Promised Land.

That is when Satan will most viciously oppress you, most powerfully oppose you, and intensify his efforts to lead you astray. To seek an abundant spiritual life is to feel the fangs of the serpent. The victorious Christian must win out over the devil!

In my last pastorate I led my church toward the Promised Land without preparing them for the warfare. With evidences of genuine revival all around us, the devil got right in the middle of it all and attacked. Satan sowed a whole crop of frictions, misunderstandings, difficulties, and divisions before we became aware of him. I baptized three hundred new members and cauterized the wounds of three hundred old members, all in the same church and in the same year.

Then God taught me about spiritual warfare. I immediately preached a series of sermons on our satanic adversary and on how to defeat him. I must have preached about Satan for an entire summer. While I was preaching that series of sermons, I recall a young boy calling out to me one Sunday evening to say: "Are we having the devil again tonight, preacher?" We had the devil around there for months. But we learned about the warfare, and then God blessed in a greater fashion. The devil did not leave; he came on more persistently. But we were not so easily deceived. We began resisting him, and some folks made the Promised Land.

A young deacon in that church made an interesting comment: "Preacher, God could not afford to send real revival to most of our American churches. We would not know how to handle it. His blessings would draw the attention of Satan, who would tear a church apart that did not recognize him or resist him!"

To lead you into the Promised Land, God must prepare you for spiritual conquest. Therefore, between "Egypt" and "Canaan" there is always a "wilderness."

The wilderness was God's training ground to prepare Israel for the warfare. He prepared them through testing: "And thou shalt remember all the way which the Lord thy God led thee these forty years in the wilderness, to humble thee, and

to prove [test] *thee,* to know what was in thine heart, whether thou wouldest keep his commandments, or no" (Deut.
8:2, italics added). To prove means to test. To tempt is also
a means of testing (Gen. 22:1). The words "prove," "tempt,"
and "test" are used synonymously in the Scriptures.

The wilderness is for testing. It is a time when your com-
mitment will be tested to its limit. It is a period of spiritual
development which you desperately need to understand.

The key to a full understanding of trial, or temptation, is to
see the experience as a synchronization of three separate acts.
It usually consists of an action by Satan, an action by God,
and an action by man.

Satan's Wiles

You will never be ready for the fullness of God's promises
until you are prepared for conflict with the devil. Satan ab-
hors all that pleases God, and he never misses a chance to
snare God's best.

One of the most distinguishing marks of our day — estab-
lishing it as a day of renewed spiritual insight — is the attention
Christians are giving to the study of Satan. His greatest
weapon against you is blindness to his existence. Satan is real.
He opposes every spiritual life. But "we are not ignorant of
his devices" (2 Cor. 2:11). Satan has two basic forms of
attack:

Satan uses oppression. One of the basic methods with which
Satan opposes a dedicated Christian life is by oppression. Suddenly, ferociously, with a vicious and malign intent, Satan
will pounce upon you: "Be careful — watch out for attacks
from Satan, your great enemy. He prowls around like a
hungry, roaring lion, looking for some victim to tear apart.
Stand firm when he attacks. Trust the Lord; and remember
that other Christians all around the world are going through
these sufferings too" (2 Pet. 5:8-9, TLB).

When Satan attacked Job, storms raged, thieves moved in to
steal, lightning fell from the sky, sickness befell him. Think of
it! Satan had power to send all of this (Job 1:13 to 2:7).

Satan attacks from without to oppress you. He sends calamity. These afflictions are designed to discourage. He would "drive you to drink." He would plunge you into despair!

Satan uses suggestion. The most common weapon Satan employs, however, is his power of suggestion. This attack is within. He invades your mind. This was his method in the Garden of Eden. Listen to his suggestions for Eve: "Hath God said . . . ye shall not surely die . . . God doth know that in the day ye eat thereof, then your eyes shall be opened, and ye shall be as gods" (Gen. 3:1-5).

It is as if Satan whispers in your ear. Throughout the centuries, men have acted rashly, spoken hastily, thought incorrectly, doubted needlessly, desired lustfully, grasped greedily, coveted incessantly — all in response to satanic suggestion. For example, Satan accuses you to fill you with false guilt.

Satan also has certain clever lines which he has sown into the thinking of mankind. His standard remarks include such thoughts as: Why don't you hit him in the nose? Demand your rights; don't let him treat you like that! Go ahead and do it; nobody will ever know. People might think you are a fanatic. Go ahead and try just one! I do not know how Satan triggers such thoughts — maybe by posthypnotic suggestion so that certain thoughts will be triggered by certain circumstances. Maybe his demonic spirits are always present to plant such thoughts. Maybe these thoughts result from the evil bent of that "old nature" you inherit, which inevitably produces certain behavioral response patterns. Maybe all three! One thing is certain. The thoughts arise and behind it all is a personal evil force in this world which you would be most foolish to ignore!

God's Withholding

Although Satan can do horrible things, that is not to say he can do anything. Satan can do nothing except what God allows. Sometimes God intercedes! In fact, God prevents Satan from doing anything to a Christian that cannot be worked into some good purpose (Rom. 8:28).

God plays a part in every testing experience. God does not allow Satan a free hand at testing you. He never allows Satan to test you beyond the limit of your endurance. "There hath no temptation [testing] taken you but such as is common to man: but God is faithful, who will not suffer you to be tempted [tried] above that ye are able . . . to *bear* it" (1 Cor. 10:13, italics added).

God withholds his protection. Consider the synchronization of a testing experience, noting the interaction between God and Satan. Satan will seek to oppress you, but he succeeds only when God withholds his protection. For example, as God led the children of Israel out of Egypt, he temporarily withheld his protection of them: "And the Lord hardened the heart of Pharaoh king of Egypt, and he pursued after the children of Israel . . . all the horses and chariots of Pharaoh, and his horsemen, and his army, and overtook them encamping by the sea" (Ex. 14:8-9).

However, as I said, God withheld his protection temporarily. Later, he delivered them (Ex. 14:16-18). But that temporary withholding of all visible protection was enough to test the mettle of Israel's faith, which was weak.

And when Pharaoh drew nigh, the children of Israel lifted up their eyes, and, behold, the Egyptians marched after them; and they were sore afraid: and the children of Israel cried out unto the Lord . . . because there were no graves in Egypt, hast thou taken us away to die in the wilderness? Wherefore hast thou dealt with us, to carry us forth out of Egypt? . . . For it had been better for us to serve the Egyptians, than that we should die in the wilderness (Ex. 14:10-12).

God withholds his provision. Here again, see the delicate synchronization in the testing experience. Satan's insidious suggestions seem to be most effective when God has seemingly withheld the provision of some need he has promised in the Bible to meet. It is when something has been withheld from you that your self-centered "flesh" is most likely to rise at the suggestion: "It is not fair that you be treated like this. Where are your rights!"

For example, not long after the children of Israel escaped from Egypt they ran out of food. God temporarily withheld any provision on his part until later. However, their temporary lack of food was enough to test their faith. But they flunked their faith test: "And the whole congregation of the children of Israel murmured against Moses and Aaron in the wilderness. . . . Would to God we had died by the hand of the Lord in the land of Egypt, when we set by the flesh pots, and when we did eat bread to the full; for ye have brought us forth into this wilderness, to kill this whole assembly with hunger" (Ex. 16: 2-3).

When they should have expressed faith in God, Israel displayed a satanic attitude and murmured against him. Surely Satan was there, suggesting negative thoughts and doubts the instant there was no visible provision.

Therefore, we see the interaction of God and Satan in our testing experience: Satan sends oppression — God withholds protection; Satan makes suggestions — God withholds provision.

I have observed an inevitable result of God's withholding either protection or provision: You tend to lose the consciousness of his presence. This was a basic problem with the children of Israel in the wilderness. They tempted God presumptuously, hastily demanding that God meet some need before he was ready, because they weren't sure of his presence (Ex. 17:7; Num. 14:22). Countless are the times when I have had the privilege of counseling Christians only to hear them complain that God seemed a hundred miles away. This left them deeply discouraged, sometimes fearful, in a pit of despair. Further discussion most often revealed God had merely withheld some protection or provision, and Satan was harrassing them. Therefore, God seemed less close. They lost the sense of His presence. But they weren't abandoned, nor had they drifted away from God. They were merely going through a time of testing. Once they realized this, their spirits lifted immediately. After all, God only tests to prepare us for higher ground. "Wherein ye greatly rejoice, though now for a season, if need be, ye are in heaviness through manifold temptation. That the trial of your faith . . . might be found unto praise and love and glory at the appearing of Jesus Christ" (1 Pet. 1:6-7).

Man's Will

Even though God's withholding paves the way for Satan's wiles, your response determines whether the testing time will make you or break you. It is as you *will*. If you will respond properly, the testing will but prove or improve you! Satan dangles the bait, but you can resist. It is only when you take hold that Satan gets his hook in you!

Your will plays a part in every testing process. This is precisely why God tests: To humble you and prove how you will respond. "To prove thee, to know what was in thine heart, whether thou wouldst keep his commandments, or no" (Deut. 8:2).

I recall my first bicycle. It is one of the clearest memories of my boyhood. I had the bicycle only a few weeks when a tire went flat. The sight of that flat tire filled me with horror. I thought it meant the wheel must be replaced.

I was greatly relieved when my father said he could fix it. I recall how he took that wheel off and delivered it into the hands of a husky service station owner. The service man proceeded to take the inner tube out of the tire and fill it with air. The inner tube became so full I was afraid it would burst. Then I learned he had inflated it in order to test it. He listened for the weak spot and marked it.

Then my father brought it home, deflated the tube, patched up the weak area, and replaced it. Soon the wheel was back on my bicycle, and I was on the road again!

In exactly the same manner, God tests the very "inner tube" of your life. There are times he will turn you over to Satan, so to speak. He will allow Satan to pressure you to the bursting point in order to point out where your weak spots are. These times can be deeply distressing. Some of these testing times are so crucial you could wish yourself dead. But the testing times humble you and reveal where the weak spots are in your life.

Now let me summarize with some observations about the spiritual life drawn from the perspective of this chapter.

Between Egypt and Canaan there is always a wilderness. Merely because you have come out of spiritual Egypt does not qualify you for the Promised Land! This is not to belittle the victory of your deliverance from Egypt. Having escaped Egypt, you have already taken two giant strides forward in your spiritual development: You have died to yourself and you have been filled with the Spirit. But this only prepares you for the wilderness.

Now this ought to be magnificent news to many. How many hundreds of people have been filled with the Spirit only to enter the most severe and difficult time of their lives. The whole world might fall in around your shoulders! You have joined "the company of the committed," and Satan is out to get you.

Never let this detain you. God allows this satanic attack. He is but taking you through your wilderness. Let God use each crisis to humble you and to reveal the weak spots in your life. Get victory in every area until every major weakness (snare) is removed and you develop a balanced spiritual life. Then God will take you on into the Promised Land and to the life you have always longed for!

Once you recognize a weakness, appropriate Christ's strength for that area of your life. God will patch it up and send you on your way . . . toward the Promised Land. Like everyone else, you have certain weak spots in your life where obedience to God comes hardest and where you are more susceptible to Satan's wiles. The Scriptures refer to these as "snares of the devil," where you are "taken captive by him at his will" and from which you must "recover yourself" (2 Tim. 2:26).

God tests you to reveal every vantage point Satan has in your life. Paul emphasized the importance of knowing "the proof of you, whether ye be obedient in all things . . . lest Satan should get an advantage" (2 Cor. 2:9,11).

These snares give Satan an advantage. They are pockets of potential rebellion wherein Christ must be reinstated as Lord. When God rids you of every major snare and your life is spiritually balanced, you are ready to leave the wilderness, having "wholly followed the Lord" (Deut. 1:36).

You see, in the Promised Land, God entrusts you with power and many splendored blessings. You begin to wield considerable influence upon others. Therefore, God cannot afford to lead you into such blessings if Satan still has a snare within you, wherein he can trap you in sin and take you captive at his will. Too many people would be hurt by your fall!

Such is the meaning of this passage in reference to Satan: "Or else how can one enter into a strong man's house, and spoil his goods, except he first bind the strong man? and then he will spoil his house" (Matt. 12:29).

The strong man is bound when there is nothing in you which will respond. After binding the strong man, you are prepared to enter and spoil that which he has possessed. You can be entrusted with the power to seek healing for those he has made sick, to set at liberty those he has bound in sin, and you can be entrusted with all the miraculous power and provision of the Promised Land, to the glory of God. Hallelujah! !

Let me be quick to add that arrival in the Promised Land does not mean you arrive at a level of sinless perfection. There will be barren areas in the Promised Land stage of your spiritual development, where your life will be tested. Satan will always contest you at your most vulnerable point, and hammer away at these old weak spots. He will also press you to create a weakness in some other spot. Satan will always be seeking to set some snare in your life! But your first wilderness experience will be the most severe, through which God seeks to balance your spiritual life, and deliver you from your most besetting (often repeated) sins.

Scene 7
The Way Through the Wilderness
"How to Break the Power of Besetting Sin"

The curtain again opens to reveal Israel's journey through the wilderness.

The children of Israel have reached the desert now. It is a riverbed bleached like white bones. All sights, shapes, sounds and colors have become sterile. Distances are deceiving. A pebble, only a few feet away, might appear like a boulder. Small hills in the distance appear like the waves of a sea. Apart from the bleating of herded sheep, the occasional grunt of a camel, and the faint murmur of voices along the caravan, there would be no sound. As far as the eye can see there is only parched desert and scorched thorn trees. Occasionally, faraway across the desert, a faint column of dust can be seen above another caravan.

The children of Israel have lost all sense of the passing of time. The sun rises like a red ball and sets to release chilly night winds. But the Israelites are aware only of their hunger for some resting place.

The wilderness is certainly no place to live. It exists. It has its purpose. It serves as a demarcation point between Egypt and the Promised Land. But it is unfit for human habitation. The wilderness is to be traversed. It is the kind of country you travel through. It is fraught with danger. It is alien to life. It is a weary journey, hard going much of the way. It turns back all but the truly committed. In itself it is a test.

This is what was set forth in the last chapter: The wilderness is our testing ground. God led the children of Israel through the wilderness in order to test their obedience. He made this clear to them from the beginning. Only three days' journey beyond the Red Sea God told them what he required: "If thou wilt diligently hearken to the voice of the Lord thy God, and wilt do that which is right in his sight, and wilt give ear to his commandments, and keep all his statutes" (Ex. 15: 26). They were to obey.

On their very next journey, during the second month following their escape from Egypt, God demanded their obedience again: "That I may prove them, whether they will walk in my law, or no" (Ex. 16:4). During the third month of their journey, God asked them to obey again: "Now therefore, if ye will obey my voice indeed, and keep my covenant, then ye shall be a peculiar treasure unto me above all people" (Ex. 19:5). Remember that Israel had been obedient enough to be delivered from Egypt: "Thus did all the children of Israel; as the Lord commanded Moses and Aaron, so did they. And it came to pass that selfsame day, that the Lord did bring the children of Israel out of the land of Egypt" (Ex. 12:50-51). But this generation of Israelites never did enter the Promised Land because they never would fully obey (Num. 14:22-24).

In terms of a previous illustration, they had cut off the root stock, but some suckers needed pruning. They were generally obedient, but not totally so. They obeyed God, to a point. The wilderness uncovered certain weak spots in their lives where the devil had them snared. For example, they still murmured and complained at hardship (Ex. 16:2-3). They lusted (Num. 11:4). They turned again to idols (Ex. 32:1). These were besetting, oft-recurring sins which that generation never conquered.

Do you still have weak spots in your life where obedience is impossible, in your own strength? That's what the wilderness is for, to reveal these major weaknesses. Unlike Israel, you can get victory in these areas. Once you recognize a weakness, you can go to God who will strengthen that area of your life. He will "patch it up" and send you on your way toward the Promised Land.

The wilderness is not only for testing; it is also for triumph. Your weaknesses are manifest with the purpose of conquering them. The wilderness is for triumph in that it is the period when you should develop full obedience.

The question is how. How do you fully obey? How do you get victory over besetting sins? How do you rid yourself of disobedience? How do you clean out every pocket of rebellion and bind the devil from your life?

The sixth chapter of Romans was written to teach you how! It is the greatest passage in the Bible on how to secure victory over besetting sins. You must study it thoroughly.

To begin with, the chapter establishes God's promise to set you free from enslavement to any sin: "Knowing this, that our old man is crucified with him . . . that henceforth we should not serve sin" (Rom. 6:6). "Let not sin therefore reign" (Rom. 6:12). "For sin shall not have dominion over you (Rom. 6:14).

First let me point out what this passage does not say. It does not promise a state of sinless perfection. It does not say you will never sin again. The Bible speaks very specifically about that matter: "If we say we have no sin, we deceive ourselves, and the truth is not in us" (1 John 1:8).

Nevertheless, to my utter amazement, what it does promise is freedom from besetting sin! You never need to be a servant (slave) to any sin. There is no sin that can reign in your life. No sin shall have dominion over you. There is no sin over which you cannot triumph on your way into the Promised Land. You see, it is not the occasional sin that defeats a Christian. It is when you come to confess a sin that you committed yesterday — and the day before and the day before that — that you have a hard time believing God will forgive. This is the sin that weakens your faith, deadens your conscience, and shatters your testimony. And the Bible promises triumph over these. Think of it! There is no habit which cannot be broken. There is no temptation you cannot resist. There is no weakness you cannot overcome! But you must know this: "Knowing this, that our old man is crucified with him" (Rom. 6:6).

Think with me. As previously mentioned, you were saved

by accepting Christ's death as payment for your sins. He died your death, in your stead. Paul established this in the previous chapter: "But God commendeth his love toward us, in that, while we were yet sinners, Christ died for us" (Rom. 5: 8).

Then, in chapter six Paul elaborates further to assure us our old nature was included: "Our old man is crucified with him" (Rom. 6:6). Do you see it! When Christ died for you, the self-centered aspect of your inner nature ("flesh" or "old man") was nailed to the cross. God wants you to know this. Therefore, since Jesus died your death, you are potentially dead to sin. The potentiality becomes a reality in your daily experience when you appropriate this promise by faith. This is referred to as an "identification" truth.

You should know this. It is the very truth baptism symbolizes: You die to the old man and arise to walk in newness of life (Rom. 6:2-5).

Someone might ask, "How much triumph can we have?" You can be set completely free from every sin that snares you: "He that is dead is free from sin." Dead means unresponsive. A corpse never responds to stimuli! God will set you free from every recurring, habitual sin. The wilderness is for triumph. It represents the period in which God sets you free from besetting sins.

How do you become obedient to each command? May I suggest this biblical formula. You must obey with yieldedness, by reckoning, through the Spirit, from the heart.

With yieldedness. You become dead to sin from a position of yieldedness: "Neither yield ye your members as instruments of unrighteousness into sin: but yield yourselves unto God, as those that are alive from the dead, and your members as instruments of righteousness unto God" (Rom. 6:13).

You make Christ Lord by yielding all you are, to all he wants of your life. You give your life away one day at a time. You commit yourself to act as he directs, in dependence upon him, throughout the day.

Furthermore, the verse said you were to yield your "members" as "instruments." Your "members" refer to your feet, your hands, your lips, your eyes, your mind, your emotions, and your will. An "instrument" is a tool which is used for a specific purpose. The verse refers to specifics. You will go throughout the day keeping your members available for specific tasks.

At the very impulse of his bidding, your hands will reach out, your feet will go, or your lips will speak. I am not suggesting that you merely begin the day by saying, "I yield," then set about to do whatever you wish. This verse is talking about a daily routine of being instantly obedient to specific tasks the Lord impresses you to do. Having surrendered all rights to your life, you do what he leads, following one impulse at a time.

If he impresses you to witness to someone, your lips will speak. If you feel led to go aside to pray, your knees will bend. If God impresses you to give your employer that extra effort, your hands will busy themselves.

Also, an instrument is a tool which is used by another. Likewise, when you yield your life to obey, this does not imply that you will be doing it for God or apart from God. To the contrary, to yield is to respond in dependence upon God, so that he is doing it through you!

Specific obedience in most things is the first big step toward victory over disobedience in any one thing: "Walk in the Spirit, and ye shall not fulfil the lust of the flesh" (Gal. 5:16). You die to besetting sin from a position of yieldedness.

By reckoning. The key to it all is reckoning yourself dead: "Likewise reckon ye also yourselves to be dead indeed unto sin" (Rom. 6:11). Reckon is a faith word; it means to rely on. You bow your head and pray, "Lord, I reckon myself dead to this sin." Name it and choose to be dead to it. Be audacious enough to reckon yourself dead to a sin, just because the Bible says you are!

Through the Spirit. The overall context of this passage includes chapter eight where Paul adds: "If ye through the Spirit do mortify [put to death] the deeds of the body, ye shall live [gain spiritual life] (Rom. 8:13).

I once had a little dog named Puff. Puff ran into the street one day, was struck by a passing automobile, and was seriously injured. The accident changed his disposition. A few days later some children ran across our yard, and Puff ran after them. He bit one of them. So we took our little pet to a veterinarian, who informed us our dog was so seriously injured that his disposition would never improve. In fact, he would soon die. His advice was to put the dog to death. But we couldn't do that! We loved him too much. "No," he remarked, "you don't understand. I will put him to death for you, but you must be willing to give me the word."

Face it, your "old nature" loves that besetting sin. You enjoy it too much to quit. But the Holy Spirit will put you to death "when you are willing." Therefore, after having prayed: "Lord, I reckon myself dead to this sin," you must add these words: "And I trust the Holy Spirit to carry out the execution."

Never forget the Holy Spirit is God. He must be honored as God. He will not barge into your life any more than Jesus did. Jesus became your Savior because you asked him. He didn't burst crudely into your life, uninvited. Neither will the Holy Spirit minister uninvited. You must honor him by requesting his various ministries.

From the heart. Lastly, you must respond "from the heart." Paul said: "But God be thanked, that ye were the servants of sin, but ye have obeyed from the heart" (Rom. 6:17).

The heart is the seat of your mental, emotional, and volitional natures. Therefore, to obey from the heart means to have your mind, will, and emotions involved in obedience.

(1) Mind. There is a state of mind necessary for those who would die to sin. Peter spoke of it: "Forasmuch then as Christ hath suffered for us in the flesh, arm yourselves likewise with the same mind: for he that hath suffered in the flesh hath ceased from sin" (1 Pet. 4:1).

This is the state of mind required. God will set you free from sin, sometimes instantaneously. At other times, there will be withdrawal pains. According to the previous verse, he that hath "ceased from sin" will have suffered. If you ever die to your besetting sins, you must have a mind to suffer. You must want to be set free, even if it hurts!

(2) Emotion. How many times have people stepped forward in a worship service, emotionally moved to give up some sin, only to go right back to it later. However, there is a higher emotion, a love for our Lord, that causes us to keep his commandments, and they cease to be grievous (1 John 5:2). The only way to become dead — without response — to a besetting sin is from a motive of love for the Lord. You do it for him! You want this sin out of your life because it casts reflection upon him.

(3) Will. I have heard dozens of people criticize this emphasis of "depending upon God." "This will cause a person to sit down and expect God to do it all," they complain. Granted, passivity is a natural danger for all who cease to serve in their own strength. Once you are so released to God that he begins to work through you, your life will multiply in effectiveness. You tend to say: "Well, I don't want to serve in my own strength. I have learned the futility of that. So I will sit back and let God do it." You can draw back so far out of God's way that you cease to be involved. You reach a state of passivity. You become so heavenly minded you are of no earthly use.

Typical of such thinking is the statement, "Just get out of God's way and let him do it." But God refuses to do it, apart from you. You don't "get out of God's way." You seek to find his way, then get right in the middle of it, asking God to do it all through you.

Anybody who is supposed to have entered the deeper spiritual life and is doing less for God than before has never experienced true spirituality. Such have forgotten what I call the yoke principle: "Come unto me, *all ye that labour and are heavy laden,* and I will give you rest. *Take my yoke upon you,* and learn of me; for I am meek and lowly in heart: and ye shall find rest unto your souls. *For my yoke is easy, and my burden is light"* (Matt. 11:28-30, italics added).

You take his yoke when you serve in cooperation (yoked) with him. You do not go it alone. Nor do you expect him to do it without you. But you serve together with — yoked with — in cooperation with him.

A yoke was a large, wooden instrument, heavy in itself; yet it lessened the burden of two oxen because they pulled together rather than against one another. It is worth noticing, also, that the yoke sides were uneven. One was larger so the strong ox could bear the greater part of the load. That is Christ's side.

Those deeply spiritual believers will "labor" but not be "heavy laden." They won't be trying to do it all alone, in their own strength. They will exert themselves but in dependence on him: "Whereunto I also labour, striving according to his working, which worketh in me mightily" (Col. 1:29).

It is so with your victory over sin. You reckon yourself dead to a specific sin. You do so in dependence upon the Holy Spirit. *But you also do all you can to resist temptation.* You exercise all the willpower you can to withstand. Paul blamed the Hebrews because: "Ye have not resisted unto blood, striving against sin" (Heb. 12:4).

But you have given your all before, in attempts to quit a sin, and it proved hopeless. The difference now is that you do it by faith, claiming a definite biblical promise, and depending upon his Spirit.

Therefore, you must reckon yourself dead, in dependence upon the Holy Spirit and from a position of yieldedness (willing to do what he leads), but exerting all your willpower, "resisting unto blood, striving against sin!"

Your will is involved!

In summary, may I remind you that all I have done is lift four phrases right out of Scripture to suggest you become obedient: with yieldedness (Rom. 6:13); by reckoning (Rom. 6:11); through the Spirit (Rom. 8:13); and from the heart (Rom. 6:17).

In the First Baptist Church of Fairview Heights, Illinois, where I was pastor, we had a member of that church named Lee Maurer. Frankly, he was not too popular with me. He was a rough railroad engineer who had little time for God. He would come and teach a Sunday School class of boys on Sunday morning, then skip the worship service and walk on home. He would not stay and hear me preach!

How many times I had slipped into my study to prepare my heart prior to the preaching service. I would kneel in prayer, arise to preach with my heart all atune, only to have it thrown out of tune as I glanced out my study window to see Lee walking home again, not staying for the preaching service. What a jarring note that struck within me!

One morning Lee accidentally overheard a conversation between his two boys and one of their friends. "I don't know why we shouldn't smoke," the friend told his boys. "Your dad does, and he teaches a Sunday School class down at the church!"

That statement hit Lee with tremendous force. He felt the only way he would ever keep his sons in school was to keep them playing football. But our coach had a strict rule: Nobody could smoke and play football. Furthermore, Lee had counted on the church to keep his boys clean. Would his own influence counteract that?

Later that same day Lee was still worrying a little about the effect his smoking would have upon his boys. Then the deeper thought struck him, "Yes, and what reflection will it cast on my Lord?" In that instant Lee Maurer became convicted smoking was wrong for him. But he had tried to quit smoking no less than a dozen times without success. He was a "chain" smoker, and that chain kept him bound.

That next Sunday morning Lee remained for our preaching service. In the providence of God, I was preaching on Romans 6. I kept repeating God's promise: There is no sin which can have dominion over a Christian.

After the service, Lee asked to speak privately with me. I knew he must really have a problem if he stayed for the preaching service, so we went immediately back to my study.

He related the story about smoking and shared his conviction. Then he asked, "Does Romans 6 teach that God will give me the power to quit smoking?"

"Well, no, he won't do it for you," I replied.

"What do you mean?" he said. "You just spent thirty minutes proclaiming this victory is for everyone."

"No, not for you, Lee," I insisted. "Don't you recall I said you had to seek this victory from a position of yieldedness." Then I went on to remark that surely his life wasn't yielded. The only time he ever showed up at church was for Sunday School. He wouldn't stay for preaching service. And then I elaborated upon a few other choice things I knew as his neighbor!

I will never forget it. Lee pounded his fist down on my desk and said, "All right — I yield!" I knew he meant it!

He took the cigarettes out of his pocket and tossed them over on my desk. We knelt down together, and Lee prayed something like this:

Lord, I don't fully understand all this, but I know that smoking is wrong for my life, and I have always believed the Bible. Therefore, I reckon myself dead to this sin just because the Bible tells me I am. I am ready to die, regardless of the pain. So, I reckon, I reckon, I reckon. I reckon it done! Oh, yes, and Lord, I trust the Holy Spirit to carry out the execution. In Jesus' Name I pray, Amen!

After we arose from prayer, I encouraged Lee to pray the same prayer each morning and assured him I would be doing the same.

Monday night Lee gave me a telephone call to inform me he had made it through the entire day without smoking a single cigarette. "I didn't smoke a cigarette," he said, "but I chewed twelve packages of gum!" Tuesday night he called to report another successful day. He was exuberant!

Wednesday night he phoned me to give the same victorious report. That day his fireman had been sick, and the substitute fireman was a compulsive smoker. Lee said, "Smoke was every-where. There was more smoke inside our engine than there was coming out of the smokestack. There were times the smell of cigarette smoke made me think I would die without one, but there was always a switching station that diverted my at-tention, a Scripture verse, or I would be sharing my faith with the fellow and ashamed to ask for one." God saw me through, and I didn't sneak one puff."

So went the days, and by Sunday Lee Maurer was thrilled out of his mind. You see, for the first time since the first sweet days of his conversion, Lee Maurer had become aware that God was real! He had actually experienced God's power, and he never got over it! When a man touches fire, he can never again doubt that fire burns.

Lee now knew that God was alive within his life, and he set about seeking all God had for him. Soon he became a leader in our church.

One day, about two months later, I heard a knock upon my study door. It was Lee. He stood there with a huge Bible under his arm and said: "Well, preacher, I have decided to take a night shift at work so I can go visiting with you this afternoon. We will go and tell people about Jesus and how God can meet their deepest needs." I won't attempt to describe Lee's ap-pearance in those days. But I all but fainted at his suggestion. He wore the wildest colors. He had no time for a haircut. With that big Bible under his arm, people could spot us coming two blocks away. It looked like Elijah was by my side. I was too proud to go with him but too proud to admit I did not visit every day. So off we went. He would show up promptly, every day. He made a soul-winner out of me before it was over!

Then one day Lee arrived to say, "I don't need you any more, Preacher."

I replied with an incredulous, "What?"

"I don't need you any more. I've watched God use your approach. It's simple. Now, I'll get someone to go with me.

You get someone to go with you, and we will reach twice as many folks."

That year we baptized thirty-five new adult members into our church — adults who were led to Christ by Lee Maurer. About a year ago I telephoned him long distance and asked how things were going. "Pastor," he replied, "this is our best year ever. Lil and I were used of God to lead 105 persons to Christ in the year just ended and saw them unite with the church!"

All this because one man discovered that God was real and alive with power to those who believe!

Lee simply claimed God's promise to rid him of besetting sin. But he obeyed in the scriptural way. He died to that sin:

With yieldedness. — Remember, he slammed his fist on the desk and said, "I yield."

By reckoning. — He prayed: "I have always believed the Bible. Therefore, I reckon myself dead to that sin just because the Bible tells me I am."

Through the Spirit. — Remember, he added to his prayer, "Oh, yes, and Lord, I trust the Holy Spirit himself to carry out the execution."

From the heart. — *Mind*: He said, "I am ready to die, regardless of the pain." That's the necessary state of mind. *Emotions*: Recall the steps in his conviction. At first, smoking was wrong because of the influence upon his boys. But soon he was moved by the higher emotion of love for his Lord. *Will*: He reckoned himself dead by simply praying in faith, but he also did all he could — the first day he chewed twelve packages of gum.

Oh, the unsurpassed joy I have known in teaching people how to die. There was the teen-age boy of Guyman, Oklahoma, who died to lust. There was a preacher's wife in San Diego, California, who died to a smoking habit of twenty years. There was the winsome lady of Port Arthur, Texas, who died to complaining, the music director who died to berating his children, the crisp young housewife who died to criticism and the sins of a sharp tongue. In Maryland I saw a couple die to a deep-seated animosity. In Ohio I saw one liberated from liquor. In Georgia I saw one set free from the bondage of dope. I have seen preachers liberated from fleshly ambition and women released from worry. I have received letters from New Mexico by those who died to temper, jealousy, and hatred.

How do you get released from bondage? You must come to the place where you are willing to write out your own obituary. Survey your life; seek out your besetting sins; and die! That's it, and when you do, your whole life will move forward spiritually, right down the line. It has been said that we are not to judge ourselves by abstinance from sins for which we have no inclination. The question is, are we gaining the victory at that point where we are specially weak and assailable?

One of the unique battles of the First World War took place on the bloody fields of death in France. There were many small hills across that battlefront. "Hill Sixty" was a vital hill in the center of the battle line. When the Germans held Hill Sixty, they dominated the whole front. When the Allies held it, they dominated the entire front. The hill changed hands many times.

The Allies decided to undermine that hill and blow it up. They dug a tunnel right on through to the heart of it. Just as they were loading it with high explosives, they heard the Germans coming into the hill from the other side to do the same thing. But the allies were there first. They loaded the hill with dynamite, and put on an offensive. Then, when the counter attack came and the battle raged, they retreated. Hill Sixty was abandoned and the Germans occupied it in strength. They began to fortify it. Then the Allies stood back for the tremendous moment when a button was touched and the hill was destroyed. As the hill blew, the Allied armies charged across what had been a "no man's land," and the whole battle moved forward, right down the line. They swept forward for three miles.

Somewhere in your life is a Hill Sixty, . . . in the center of the battle line. It is a point in the battle line where you are constantly defeated. Perhaps only you and God know about it. Put a finger on that Hill Sixty in your life, and place another on Romans 6. Then say: "Here it is, Lord; destroy it." Put it to death as we have learned: with yieldedness, by faith, through the Spirit, and from the heart. When you do, the whole battle will move forward, right down the line.

As the curtain falls, your heart should long for real and thorough victory. If so, the next section will help you to survey your life, seek out your besetting sins, and die to sin.

Survey Your Life

It should not be too difficult for you to detect your prevailing sin. However, if you seem to be having difficulty, just honestly follow this little exercise. Ask yourself, the following questions:

"What do I think about most when alone? Where do my thoughts go when I let them run free? What do I miss the most when I am without it? What makes me most excited and happy when I possess it? What fault irritates me most when I am accused of it, and which sin do I most vigorously deny possessing?"

Moreover, perhaps a pedigree chart will help you recognize your prevailing sin (and sins). Our old self-centered nature is the basic cause of all sin. The self seems to spawn seven deadly species of sin. Pope Gregory the Great, in the sixth century, divided all sins under seven heads. Thomas Aquinas and most great theologians have agreed. The Scheme of Dante's "purgatory" follows his order, and they are discussed in Chaucer's "Parson's Tales" and Marlowe's "Doctor Faustus." The self seems to spawn seven deadly species of sin. These in turn, hatch out all kinds of variations:

1. Pride: vain ambition, criticism, conceit, hypocrisy, disobedience, fear, pretense, discord, do you feel sorry for yourself, are you inconsiderate, do you brag about achievements, are your feelings easily hurt, do you resent correction, do you pretend to be better than you are, are you stubborn, do you demand your own way, do you seek recognition, and so forth.

2. Avarice: covetousness, greed, fraud, perjury, dishonesty, selfishness, ingratitude, do you tell lies, cheat in school or business, do you exaggerate, do you steal, are you discontent.

3. Envy: criticism, slander, jealousy, possessiveness, is there anyone you do not like to hear praised, do you covet anything that belongs to someone else, do you gossip about others, and so forth.

4. Lust: fornication, adultery, impatience, slave to a harmful habit, are you guilty of an illicit infatuation, do you read that which stirs the passions, and so forth.

5. Anger: ill temper, vindictiveness, tantrums, quarrelsome, argumentative, revenge, bitterness, cursing, touchiness, joylessness, is there anyone you hate, do you hold a grudge, is there anyone you have hurt, are you a party to divisions, are you impatient, are you disobedient to parents, and so forth.

6. Gluttony: overeating, drunkenness, materialism, doubleminded, and all kinds of excesses.

7. Sloth: laziness, softness, idleness, indifference, procrastination, self-satisfaction, lukewarm faithlessness, has your idle talk hurt someone, do you neglect worship, Bible study, prayer, witnessing, do you grumble and complain at difficulties, do you spend too much time before a TV.

Turn to the back of the book for your Travelers Aids. Do so now. Read the section at the bottom of the first page. It is your Demolition Plan for Hill Sixtys. Use it daily as you seek out your sins and really die. Use this plan unsparingly until you are free from besetting sins!

Scene 8
The Way Out of the Wilderness
"How to Believe for a Miracle"

As the scene unfolds, the caravan of Israel is coming out of the wilderness. Behind you there is nothing but those ever-present, stunted thorn trees, covered with the dust of the desert.

You are approaching Kadesh-barnea, at the southern edge of the Promised Land. Small children gather at the roadside to watch the caravan pass. Some of the more mischievous ones fit smooth pebbles into slingshots and cause some disorder among the herds. Women bend over thornbush fires, stirring savory mixtures. A man working behind his plow stops in the midst of his furrow to watch you pass by.

You are finally arriving at a crossroad in your journey. You are arriving at Canaan's southern door, and now you will be forced to decide whether you will enter, or not!

In a little while, Joshua will step forward to present God's challenge: "We were then at Kadesh-barnea [on the border of the Promised Land] and I said to the people, 'The Lord God has given us this land. Go and possess it as he told us to. Don't be afraid! *Don't even doubt!*' " (Deut. 1:21, TLB)

Suddenly you realize that, in actuality, your decision will be based upon faith!

In a quaint little shop in Nicosia on the island of Cypress, my wife and I were leisurely searching for gifts. What caught our attention was a unique display of jewelry. Everything in the jewelry case was modestly priced. That is why my wife was so shocked when she picked up one of the smaller pieces to be told it cost about $40. But when she questioned the shopkeeper, the worth of the little item became evident as he lifted a small latch to reveal the jewel of real value within.

When you "lift the latch" of God's finest saints, you will always find one precious quality of insurpassable value — faith. A man of God is always a man of faith. All the promises of God are appropriated by faith (Heb. 6:12). The question is: What are you believing God to do?

In the final analysis, there was one reason why the children of Israel failed to enter the Promised Land — *unbelief.* Their faith was too small. One of the most significant commentaries on that Old Testament experience is found in the third chapter of Hebrews. This passage specifically states that Israel could not enter in because of unbelief: Harden not your hearts, as in the provocation, in the day of temptation in the wilderness: when your fathers tempted me, proved me, and saw my words forty years. Wherefore I was grieved with that generation, and said, They do always err in their heart. . . . Take heed, brethren, lest there be in any of you an evil heart of unbelief. . . . But with whom was he grieved forty years . . . and to whom swore he that they should not enter into his rest, but to them that believe not? So we see they could not enter in because of unbelief (Heb. 3:8-19).

You see, Israel lacked the faith to obey. Israel measured the possibility of conquering Canaan in terms of what they could do. Indeed, apart from faith in the sufficiency of God, Canaan's conquest must have appeared inconceivable — a dreamer's folly.

Obedience comes by faith. "By faith Abraham, when he was tried, offered up Isaac" (Heb. 11:17). He passed his test by faith.

Likewise, there is a profound sense in which the wilderness is not only for testing, but it was also for trusting. God tested Israel's faith to obey!

The passage in Hebrews 3 also reveals what Israel's faith lacked. Their sin was not "nonbelief," the absence of faith. Their problem was "unbelief," insufficient faith. They lacked what I choose to call "full-hearted faith." Notice the specific references to their heart: "Harden not your hearts" (Heb. 3:8). "They do always err in their heart" (Heb. 3:10). "An evil heart of unbelief" (Heb. 3:12). God tested their heart: "To prove thee, to know what was in thine heart" (Deut. 8:2).

In the Bible, the heart of man is synonymous with his soul — the seat of his emotional, mental, and volitional faculties. The following examples could be multiplied: Esther 6:6 — "Hamon thought in his heart" (seat of mind). John 16:6 — "Sorrow hath filled your heart" (seat of emotions). Isaiah 32:6 — "His heart will" (seat of will).

Therefore, full-hearted faith means to believe with your mind, your emotions, and your will. There you have the inner dynamics of faith.

If I have uncovered a deeper significance of Israel's testing, it is this: God tested the Israelites in such a way that their minds, emotions, and wills had to be involved in believing. Israel failed at each point.

From this I discovered three tests of faith that you should apply against everything you ever believe God for! What do you most want to believe God for right now? Whatever it is, concentrate on it long enough to get it fixed in your mind. But before you seek God for it, apply three tests, which are in the form of three questions. These tests will refine your faith. They will help you to develop adequate faith. They will teach you how to believe. Then you can strengthen your faith through every testing — to enter and dwell in the fullness of God's promises. Simply check for full-hearted faith to see if you are believing with mind, emotions, and will.

The Mental Test: What Do You Base It On?

The heart is the seat of man's *mind,* emotions, and will. Therefore, to believe with your heart, your mind must be involved in believing.

There is a mental aspect to faith. Your faith should be intelligent. That is, you cannot just believe God for anything or everything. There should be an intelligent basis for your belief. Test your faith with this question: What do you base it on?

Everything you believe God for must be based on some promise or principle of Scripture. God punished the Israelites because they did not enter Canaan. They were without excuse. They had a basis for believing God would give them the Promised Land. They had his word on it (Ex. 6:8).

However, I believe God knew the children of Israel would have a difficult time believing such a tremendous promise. Therefore, he tried to strengthen their faith by giving them lesser promises. For example, he tested them with a promise concerning diseases: "He proved them, and said, If thou wilt diligently hearken to the voice of the Lord . . . I will put none of these diseases upon thee, which I have brought upon the Egyptians" (Ex. 15:25-26). Next, he tested them with a promise concerning food: "Then said the Lord unto Moses, Behold, I will rain bread from heaven for you . . . that I may prove them (Ex. 16:4).

Had the children of Israel responded properly to these lesser promises, their faith would have enlarged until they could have believed God for the Promised Land itself! Faith develops that way. All Christians are given a like amount of precious faith (2 Pet. 1:1). As we exercise faith, like yeast, it enlarges, and we develop "from faith unto faith" (Rom. 1: 17).

Christian faith has an intelligent basis. It is faith in God's word. It certainly is not what some people refer to as blind faith.

An old Arab dismounted from his camel, late one evening, at the close of a weary day's journey. He took a lamp and a little knapsack, and walked over to sit in the sand. He lit his lamp. He unfolded his knapsack. Before him were three dates. This was the substance of his evening meal. He picked up the first date, held it under the lamp, and opened it — to find a worm in it. He threw it over his shoulder, out into the darkness, and reached for the second date. He held it under the lamp and opened it. To his dismay, it also had a worm in it. So he threw it back over his shoulder also, out into the darkness. He looked down at that last one for awhile. Then he leaned over and blew out his lamp, picked up the date, and ate it!

That's blind faith! But it is not characteristic of Christian faith. Christian faith is enlightened. Christian faith is always based on the light of God's Word, on a promise or principle from the Scriptures. Before we exercise faith, we must ask ourselves, "Is what I am believing God for in keeping with his Word?" Do I have an intelligent basis for my faith? Do I have a scriptural principle or promise for believing this?

One would conclude that Bible study is vital to this enlargement and excercising of our faith. We must be enlightened of his Word, if we are to base our faith upon it. That is the exact advice God gave Israel, to prepare them for the Promised Land: "This book of the law shall not depart out of thy mouth; but thou shalt meditate therein day and night, that thou mayest observe to do all that is written therein: for then thou shalt make thy way prosperous" (Josh. 1:8).

Bountiful Christians simply claim all they have Scripture for!

The Emotional Test: Why Do You Want It?

The heart is the seat of man's mind, *emotions,* and will. There, to believe with your heart, your *emotions* must be involved in believing.

There is an emotional element in faith. Therefore, faith should be motivated by the finest emotion. The highest Christian emotion is love. Faith should be motivated by love (Gal. 5:6). And the highest object of your love should be the Lord. Therefore, whatever you are believing God for, ask yourself this question: Why do you want it? Do you want it for God's sake, for the sake of those God loves, or just for yourself?

One reason God tries our faith is to refine our desire for trusting him. God wants us to trust him for his sake, not just for our sakes. Love places others first, yourself second. And God elevates our desires through trials.

Moses was led to take his prophet's rod, hold it over the Red Sea, and part the waters (Ex. 14:16). Thus, the Israelites passed through on dry ground while the water reconverged upon the pursuing army. But the motive of Moses was not just to save himself. God had given him a higher motive: "And the Egyptians shall know that I am the Lord, when I have gotten me honour upon Pharaoh, upon his chariots, and upon his horsemen" (Ex. 14:18). Moses did it for the glory of God!

Before you act in faith, examine your emotions and ask yourself: Do I want this for my good, or to bring him glory! God demands that you love him enough to consider your trials as opportunities to trust him — for your good and his glory.

But the Israelites viewed their trials as threats, rather than opportunities. About forty-five days into the wilderness, the children of Israel found themselves without food. The test was on! But they viewed it with alarm: "Would to God we had died by the hand of the Lord in the land of Egypt . . . When we did eat bread to the full; for ye have brought us forth into this wilderness, to kill this whole assembly with hunger." (Ex. 16:3)

This was certainly not a response of love. They considered their test a threat. They lacked the love to trust him. So, "They steeled themselves against his love and complained against him in the desert while he was testing them" (Heb. 3: 8, TLB).

God tests the emotional element of your faith: Do you want it for his glory, or just for yourself? Paul learned to: "take pleasure in infirmities, in reproaches, in necessities, in persecutions, in distresses for Christ's sake (2 Cor. 12:10).

Peter also taught that our faith would be tried for God's glory. "Beloved, think it not strange concerning the fiery trial which is to try you, as though some strange thing happened to you. But rejoice . . . that when his glory shall be revealed" (1 Pet. 4:12-13).

Whatever you believe God for, want it for him. Your greatest good is to bring him glory. Men of God have accomplished epic feats of faith in times past. But the emotional desire that motivated their faith was pure: They acted for the glory of God.

In another Old Testament experience, the Philistines were

encamped on one mountain and the Israelites on the other. A valley lay between them. The giant Goliath came down into the valley, cursing God and challenging an Israelite to meet him in combat. For forty days Goliath challenged Israel. The giant had stalked into the valley, twice each day, defying the Israelites and their God. Finally, David arrived on the scene. Immediately he responded with indignation: "Who is this un-circumcised Philistine, that he would defy the armies of the living God" (1 Sam. 17:26)? In a classic showdown, with intense drama, young David came down the mountain and out into the valley. He had faith that five little stones and a slingshot were more than a match for a giant armed with sword, spear, and shield. He believed: "The Lord will deliver thee into mine hand." But he was moved by proper desire. He stalked down the mountainside, stating his motivation: "That all the earth may know that there is a God in Israel" (1 Sam. 17:46). His desire was for the glory of God.

In yet another Old Testament situation, Elijah had his show-down with the priests of Baal on Mount Carmel. With a mo-mentous demonstration of faith, he called down fire from heav-en. But when praying for God to answer by fire, he empha-sized it was in order to: "Let it be known this day that thou art God in Israel . . . that this people may know that thou art the Lord God" (1 Kings 18:36-37).

To enlarge your faith, view every problem situation as an opportunity to express your love by trusting God to work it out for his glory and your good. You must want to trust him. Never mumble! Never grumble! Never gripe! Never mur-mur! Never complain!

The Will Test: How Do You Express It?

The heart is the seat of man's mind, emotions, and *will*. Therefore, to believe with your heart, your *will* must be in-volved in believing.

There is an exercise of the will in an expression of genuine Christian faith. There is always something you are to do in order to express your faith. God led the Israelites through the wilderness to test their *will*: "God led thee these forty years in the wilderness . . . to prove [test] thee, to know what was in thine heart, whether thou wouldest keep his commandments or no" (Deut. 8:2). Would they obey? You see, biblical faith requires an action of the will. Your will must be involved in believing. Before you believe God for anything, ask yourself this question: How do you express it? There is always something to be done as an expression of your faith!

The eleventh chapter of Hebrews is often referred to as the "Royal Roll Call of Faith." It lists the greats — those who have distinguished themselves by their faith, down through the annals of Old Testament history. But notice they expressed their faith by an *act of their will*:

By faith Abel offered a sacrifice (v. 4).
By faith Noah prepared an ark (v. 7).
By faith Sara delivered a child (v. 11).
By faith Abraham offered up Isaac (v. 17).
By faith Isaac blessed Jacob and Esau (v. 20).
By faith Jacob blessed both sons of Jacob (v. 21).
By faith Joseph gave commandments (v. 22).
By faith Moses kept the passover (v. 28).
By faith the Israelites encompassed Jericho (v. 30).
By faith Rahab received the spice (v. 31).

In every case, faith was expressed by an act of the will. In biblical faith you must want to believe, you must give mental assent, but you must also exercise your will. You take an action to display your faith.

Ten lepers came to Jesus because they wanted to be healed. They mentally believed he could heal them — that is why they called out. But healing did not come until they took willful action to demonstrate their faith. God told them to go and tell the priest they were healed. The Bible says, "as they went, they were cleansed" (Luke 17:14). Healing came at the point of their action! Think about it. They would have appeared mighty foolish if God had not come through: Telling the priest something had happened, when, after all, it never did! But that is when God fulfills your faith, when you get in so deep he has to!

When I first realized how to exercise full-hearted faith, I was deeply engrossed in a Christian project. In order to complete the project, I needed $700. But I lacked the faith to believe God for it. How well I recall the determination with which I put my faith to the test. I was adequately involved emotionally. I could honestly say I wanted the $700 for the sake of God's cause, not just for my own sake. I had an intelligent basis for my faith in that I was deeply convinced the following promise had reference to my need: "But my God shall supply all your need according to his riches in glory by Christ Jesus" (Phil. 4:19).

My motive was right and I had a scriptural basis for my faith, but I had not believed with my will. I made a telephone call and sealed the matter as if the $700 were already mine. I told my wife the money was on the way. As a friend says it: "I acted as if what hadn't happened, had happened; so what hadn't happened, could happen!" Three days later I received a letter from an old friend, a physician, Dr. Robert McCall. He had not written me since college days. But there was the letter, which stated: "My wife and I were talking about you last evening, and God placed it on our hearts to have a part in your ministry. Enclosed is $100, and we will be sending $100 each month for the rest of this year. There were six months left in the year — the amount totaled $700.

I had taken action in the confidence God would provide my need — he did! God dramatically honored this step of faith. He did it to encourage me, and there have been countless blessings since — of ever-increasing magnitude.

In summary, let me remind you: It takes full-hearted faith to enter into God's fullness. God tests your obedience in such a way you must believe with your emotions, your mind, and your will. All three are imperative:

God tests your emotion: For even "though I have faith, so that I could remove mountains, and have not charity [love], I am nothing" (1 Cor. 13:2).

God tests your mind: Lest "they should believe a lie" (2 Thess. 2:11).

God tests your will: Because "faith without works is dead" (Jas. 2:26).

Is your faith too small? Because of unbelief, some never get beyond the wilderness. How many times has it been said of us, "He did not many mighty works there because of their unbelief" (Math. 13:58)? He is about mighty things today, when we believe!

The Richard Hogue team was preparing for an evangelistic crusade at the sports arena in downtown San Diego, California. It was the first religious event ever held in that arena, and anticipations were high. Our team had a strange feeling about that crusade — it had the "aura" of heaven upon it! We expected God to do things it would take the Holy Spirit to explain!

The chairman of a vital committee was a young pastor named Buster Reeves. Two months prior to the crusade I flew into San Diego for a preparation rally, and the young pastor was to meet me at the airport. Upon my arrival I was told he could not meet me because his wife was taken to the hospital for an emergency operation. She had cancer, one of the fastest growing type of tumors. Nothing could be done. The doctor gave her two months to live. There was talk about his taking a leave of absence for a few months. He could take his wife back to her native home for the last months of her life. Richard Hogue's reaction was immediate. Speaking with the pastor by telephone, he said: "God has given us a heavy burden about that crusade. We have been moved to special prayer. Surely God has mighty things in store. Is this not one thing God has been preparing us for — to believe him for a miracle of healing?

The pastor and I talked at length about it. His wife had a marvelous spirit. They decided against returning to their home in Texas. They would remain in San Diego, and he would continue his responsibilities in the church and the crusade — we would trust God to heal her.

Two months later our entire team was in San Diego, and the crusade was off to a wonderful beginning. Hundreds were making decisions for Christ. But the young minister's wife had barely made it. Her condition was poor. She could not retain her food. She was in pain. She now had two tumors, both as large as the one removed two months before.

Late Tuesday evening our team gathered in a hotel room. The pastor met with us, and we brought the matter to God. We tested ourselves with the questions considered in this chapter:

(1)   The mental test: What were we basing our prayer on?
(2)   The emotional test: Why did we want God to do it?
(3)   The will test: How were we expressing our faith?

In each case our faith seemed solid!

Emotionally, we had reached a state of sincerity: We wanted this healing for the glory of God and for a witness of his power, "that all may know there is yet a God." We knew this young couple was reconciled to God's will, even if it had been to the contrary.

Secondly, we felt *mentally* assured. We reviewed a scriptural promise. Again the Holy Spirit seemed to impress our hearts that: "The prayer of faith shall save the sick, and the Lord shall raise him up" (Jas. 5:15). Obviously God meant this verse to apply in some cases. We shared the deep conviction that it would, indeed, apply to this need.

Lastly, we tested our will. Had we expressed our faith in action? Yes, the young couple had continued in their ministry, just as if she were already healed. Then it dawned upon us: we had stopped trusting too soon, we simply needed to continue. So we all prayed again.

Each, in his own way, thanked God for having healed her! We left the room refusing to doubt. We left expecting! The young pastor also did a very significant thing. The next day he took his wife to the doctor for confirmation that she was healed. You can imagine the deep and boundless joy, then, when the doctor called him in to exclaim: "The tumors are gone. I cannot find them!" You can also imagine the doctor's amazement when the pastor calmly said, "I knew it!"

Of course, this young couple know the most wonderful miracle of the crusade was the salvation decisions of over fifteen hundred persons — they received eternal life! But there are times when God will bless us with multiplied blessings!

Nothing spices my life with excitement, or shatters monotony, like frequent, miraculous victories of faith. Such victories are characteristic of the Promised Land. Life there is often challenging but never dull! Therefore, the wilderness is worth it, when we really learn to trust. That is what it is for. The wilderness is for trusting.

In fact, God is forever calling our hand on this matter of faith. He inevitably brings us to some Kadesh-barnea: a point at which we must exercise our faith or miss a blessing. As the curtain closes, you are still standing at the crossroads, and God waits upon you at Kadesh-barnea, to see if you will believe him or not!

Here is what you should do. Turn to the back of the book and read the Traveler's Aid marked: "For Use in the Wilderness." This is your "Wilderness Survival Kit." It will see you through. Use is constantly. You will never be ready for the Promised Land until you are exercising great, New Testament faith!

Scene 9
The Ways of the Wanderers
"Guess Who I Saw in the Wilderness"

The curtain lifts for one last view at the wilderness. But I am immediately disconcerted by the sudden realization of one persistent impression that has been with me all along. Up until this moment it had been a lingering sensation, now it comes into conscious focus.

Throughout every mile of the journey, I have had the strange sensation of having been there before. I have seen nothing but familiar scenes. I have traveled common roads. There has always been a sense of sameness about my surroundings. Very little occurred that surprised me. It was as if I could anticipate every happening along the road. I felt like I had traveled that way a hundred times before!

In fact, the first time I stood before a congregation to share what I had seen, I began with this exclamation: "Guess who I saw in the wilderness? Me!" But I not only saw myself, I saw almost all the leaders of my church and most of the best Christians I had ever known. What a shock to discover we had been living in the wilderness all along and did not know it!

Did I see you there?

The following characteristics will typify your life if you are in the wilderness.

You Will See Some Miraculous Provisions of Need

Be careful not to mistake God's sustaining provision for his promised abundance. It is common to think you have reached the Promised Land of spiritual development while yet in a spiritual wilderness.

Seldom do I teach about the bountiful blessings of the Promised Land without conversing with someone who mistakenly thinks he is there. He will approach me after the service to remark something like this: "I know what you mean about entering the Promised Land of God's blessing. God has certainly been good to me. He has guided me all these years. I have never gone without. God has always put food on my table and clothing on my back. I remember when our Johnny was little; the doctors had almost given him up, but God miraculously healed him. I remember almost losing my business, but God came through with another miracle."

Stop right there! Review the things he mentioned: guidance, food, clothing, and miracles. These things do not designate the Promised Land. God provided this well for those in the wilderness.

They had constant guidance in the wilderness: "And the Lord went before them by day in a pillar of a cloud, to lead them the way; and by night in a pillar of fire to give them light; to go by day and night" (Ex. 13:21).

God always provided food in the wilderness: "And the children of Israel did eat manna forty years, until they came to a land inhabited; they did eat manna, until they came unto the borders of the land of Canaan" (Ex. 16:35).

They never lacked for clothing in the wilderness: "And I have led you forty years in the wilderness: your clothes are not waxen old upon you, and thy shoe is not waxen old upon thy foot" (Deut. 29:5).

God also wrought a number of miracles for the children of Israel while they were in the wilderness. For example, God parted the Red Sea for their deliverance (Ex. 14). They ran out of water, but Moses smote a rock and water came gushing forth (Ex. 17:6).

God was this good to them in the wilderness! But in the Promised Land God does more than merely guide us; he establishes us in the land. We have more than just our needs met; we prosper bountifully. Our cup runs over. God doesn't just perform miracles occasionally to deliver us from difficulty. He performs miracles constantly in the daily course of our lives.

The wilderness certainly beats Egypt. But it is a far cry from the Promised Land because you will lack the faith to appropriate God's fullness. This leads us to the next characteristic of the wilderness.

You Will Lack in Faith

The wilderness is for trusting. All those who dwell there lack in faith. There are certain aspects of life which are general symptoms of this deficiency. Ask yourself the following questions which characterize the wilderness experience.

Are you up and down? After God delivered the children of Israel through the Red Sea, they sang a special song of triumph and praise. Most of the fifteenth chapter of Exodus is used to record it. The "congregation" sang the verses, and the "Womens Missionary Society" sang the chorus (vv. 20-21). After this glorious song of vigor, vision, and victory, the Bible says: "They went three days in the wilderness, and found no water . . . and the people murmured against Moses, saying, What shall we drink?" (Ex. 15:22,24).

They were up; and three days later, they were down. All they had was "three-day faith." That was characteristic of them. They had more ups and downs than a theatergoer in an aisle seat!

How about you? Does your Christian experience vacillate? Are you a "roller coaster" Christian?

Do you tempt God? The Israelites never reached that "full assurance of faith" (Heb. 10:22). When they ran out of water the second time, they evidenced this lack of assured faith. Instead of trusting God, they chided and presumptuously demanded another miracle (Ex. 17:3). God was displeased: "And he called the name of the place Massah, and Meribah, because of the chiding of the children of Israel, and because they tempted the Lord, saying, Is the Lord among us or not?" (Ex. 17:7).

These are the "sign seekers." Lacking a faith which knows, they are never quite sure God is with them. So they constantly look for signs. Like Gideon, they are forever putting out the fleece. But they forget Gideon had to put out the fleece because he and his people were in a desperate spiritual condition. They were in a bondage like the Egyptian bondage. The miracles of God had ceased (Judg. 6:13).

I know a preacher that puts out the fleece for everything. If a pulpit committee approaches him about considering another pastorate, he will put out the fleece and say: "Lord, cause four people to respond at the invitation today. Have the music director sing a song about the cross. And I will take this as a sign you are still with me and I should stay." Don't think such a person is deeply spiritual. At this point, he is shallow. The deep Christian will not require a sign. Quite the opposite. The Bible doesn't teach us to follow signs. It teaches that signs will follow us (Mark 16:17). Thus, we are assured and will have no need for "tempted the Lord, saying, Is the Lord among us, or not" (Ex. 17:7).

It's a work of deep faith to believe God for something to happen. Some believe God only *if* something happens!

If you seek signs, your life is in the wilderness. You live too far away from God. Draw closer! The time to seek signs or put out the fleece is when you are in spiritual Egypt and you have been void of God's blessings for years.

Do you keep an idol or two? After Exodus 17 there is a parenthesis in the story of Israel's journey. Chapter after chapter is used to record the rules and laws laid down to govern Israel in the wilderness — from Exodus 17, through Leviticus, to Numbers 10.

In the midst of all this revelation, Moses was preparing to come down out of the mountain with the Ten Commandments. But the people made themselves an *idol*. The Bible says: "They have turned aside quickly out of the way which I commanded them: they made them a molten calf, and have worshipped it, and have sacrificed thereunto, and said, These be thy gods, O Israel, which have brought thee up out of the land of Egypt" (Ex. 32:8).

An idol is anything you place before God. You see, God is to be first. Anything replacing him in your interest is an idol.

It becomes your God! People in the wilderness have idols. Do you? Is there something in your life more important than God? Are there "things" you won't give up? Are there commandments you refuse to obey? God will keep you in the wilderness until you are free from every illegitimate desire. Some try to keep an idol or two!

Are you a complainer? Those in the wilderness have begun following the Lord; but they discourage easily. They have not learned patience — the ability to stay under the load and lift, until Jesus comes through. They don't really trust God. Their lack of faith is evidenced by periods of discouragement and despair.

If you recall the beginning of their journey, the Israelites had traveled but three days when they grew discouraged and "murmured" (Ex. 15:22,24). Fourteen months later they had not improved. From deep in the wilderness, God began to lead them on their journeys out (Num. 10:11,12). But they had journeyed only three days again until they fell to complaining (Num. 10:33; 11:1).

I was in the pastorate for eighteen years. For the last few years, my family and I have traveled as part of the Richard Hogue Evangelistic Team. In San Diego, a young preacher pulled me aside and said, "I am sure you really miss the pastorate, don't you?"

"There is one thing I certainly don't miss," I replied. "I certainly don't miss the constant murmuring and complaining I listened to for eighteen years!"

Some church members are about as cheerful as a graveyard on a wet Sunday. They suffer from skeptic poisoning. I've known some that have had the seven year itch, for eight years. Broadcasting on a fretwork of wrinkles, they need their faith lifted!

God promised the land of Canaan to the children of Israel. But they could not take it without a battle. God can't trust those who discourage easily (Deut. 1:21). You can count on it. Those that murmur and complain are spiritually immature.

Are you worldly? Those in the wilderness have escaped Egypt, but occasionally they long to return:

And the mixed multitude that was among them feel a lusting: and the children of Israel also wept again, and said, Who shall give us flesh to eat? We remember the fish, which we did eat in Egypt freely; the cucumbers, and the melons, and the leeks, and the onions, and the garlick: But now . . . there is nothing at all, beside the manna (Num. 11:4-6).

What a choice example! Which of us have not harbored such longing? But how few ever admit it!

How many times, as a pastor, I have come from a deacons' meeting to tell my wife: "This is the last time I am taking this monthly ride through Ulcer's Gulch. I am going to resign and take a secular job where dedication is not thwarted, but rewarded." Have you ever felt like chucking the whole Christian scene? Have you ever wanted to jettison the sacrifice and concern of the Christian life, to indulge yourself in the things of the world?

"Worldly" Christians are like this. They are not necessarily "immoral." But they live as if there were no God, as if there were no spiritual dimension of life. They live to satisfy their physical, sensual nature with the material things of life.

They also live for temporal things. That is, things that can be enjoyed here and now. Therefore, they want the things of this world, and they want them now. They want a new television set, and they want it now. They want nice clothes, and they want them now. They want a new car, and they want it now. They want a new home, and they want it now. They desire the things of this world, and they want them now. In the meantime, they don't have the time of day for God!

Let me add one comment about those times I longed for my old way of life. Inevitably, God would bring me to a more realistic perspective, and I would wonder how I could have ever entertained the thought of returning to a worldly life! Having experienced the things of Christ, how could a worldly life still be palatable? After all, without being too facetious, look what the Israelites were longing for: "cucumbers, leeks, onions, and garlick" (Num. 11:5)!

The only reason Egypt appeals to you is that you have spent too long in the wilderness. Your "manna" has grown stale! You see, the wilderness was never meant to be your permanent address. It was to be a one-way route into the Promised Land. The only reason you long for Egypt is because you live in the wilderness, and you have stayed there too long! Is this you?

Are you judgmental of others? Almost inevitably, when God's children gain release from the bondage of Egypt, they have a tendency to think themselves better than others. They become "holier-than-thou."

It seems to follow a pattern. A Christian experiences victory over sin in his life. He feels clean within. This gives him a sense of rightness with God. Being conscious of others who are yet shackled, he subconsciously feels superior. More than a few pastors have complained to me of members who have been spirit-filled, only to become loud, overbearing, judgmental, devisive, overzealous, and impatient with others. God turns them on, but they turn others off! It was so in the wilderness. For example: "And Miriam and Aaron spoke against Moses because of the Ethiopian woman whom he had married . . . and they said, Hath the Lord indeed spoken only by Moses? Hath he not spoken also by us" (Num. 12:1-2). They thought too highly of themselves, and vanity spawned criticism. How judgmental are you?

Are you fearful? At Kadesh-barnea they arrived at the threshold of the Promised Land. But they did not enter. Instead, they asked God for permission to spy out the land (Deut. 1:22). They wanted proof it was all God said it was (Deut. 1:25).

The Lord granted them permission, and Moses sent the spies in (Num. 13:17). They returned to verify the land was all God promised. They brought luscious fruit as evidence. But they told of its walled cities and mighty soldiers. Fear begets fear. Having been afraid the land was not worthy, now they were afraid they could not conquer it.

Joshua rebuked them for their fearfulness: "Only rebel not ye against the Lord, neither fear ye the people of the land . . . their defence is departed from them, and the Lord is with us: fear them not" (Num. 14:9). But they still refused to enter.

The Lord was so displeased with them He judged them. They spent a year wandering in the wilderness for every day they spied out the land. A year for each day, forty years for forty days (Num. 14:34).

You see, behind this fear was a lack of love. We trust the one we love. But when love ebbs, fear increases. Had they loved God enough, they would not have been afraid. "Perfect love casteth out fear" (1 John 4:18). Real love will wholly obey and gladly follow his command (1 John 5:3).

What about you? Are you afraid to trust God? Is that the truth about it? Are you hesitant to step out on faith in some area of God's promise? Look behind your unbelief. Is it caused by fear? Are you afraid God will not fulfill all his promises in your life? Are you afraid of looking foolish if God fails to come through? This is so often the case with unbelief. How about you?

You Are in Danger of Losing Your Inheritance

God finally gave up on the children of Israel because they stayed too long in the wilderness. God brought them up to Kadesh-barnea in one last attempt at leading them into the Promised Land. He was prepared to give it to them as an inheritance. They had faith enough to believe God didn't intend them to be enslaved, and God led them out of Egypt. But they just couldn't believe God would also be so good as to give them the finest land in the world. It was beyond their faith.

Christians are no different today. They just can't believe God will do all he has promised. Faith comes hard on an individual plain; that is, I can believe *others* have great experiences with God but have difficulty believing he would so bless me.

It was not as if they had only one chance. Kadesh-barnea was but God's last desperate effort to lead them in. It would seem they had ten times in the wilderness when God would have led them in: "Because all those men which have seen my glory, and my miracles, which I did in Egypt and in the wilderness, and have tempted me now these ten times, and have not hearkened to my voice, surely they shall not see the land" (Num. 14:22-23). Kadesh-barnea was the last straw. The promise was withdrawn. God made them spend the rest of their lives in the wilderness (Num. 14:29). Later they presumed to enter in by their own power but were unable (Num. 14:40-45). The writer of Hebrews, referring to this experience, warns us about remaining too long in the wilderness. His words are: "To day if ye will hear his voice, Harden not your hearts in the provocation, in the day of temptation in the wilderness: when your fathers tempted me, proved me, and saw my works forty years" (Heb. 3:7-9). There is a day marked against your life. If you are not out of the wilderness by that day, you will likely be too hardened to ever really trust God. Like so many thousands of others, you will spend the rest of your life wandering in a spiritual wilderness. You will never experience God's fullness on earth.

Let me be the first to admit my lack of scriptural authority for what I have just said. However, is this not the meaning of passages like the following:

Looking diligently lest any man fail of the grace of God; lest any root of bitterness springing up trouble you, and thereby many be defiled; Lest there be any fornicator, or profane person, as Esau, who for one morsel of meat sold his birthright. For ye know how that afterward, when he would have inherited the blessing, he was rejected: for he found no place of repentance, though he sought it carefully with tears (Heb. 12:15-17).

(What about Hebrews 5:11 to 6:15?)

I believe you can stay too long in the wilderness. God will revoke your birthright, and you can miss your earthly inheritance. Sometimes I wonder if this has not been the experience of the last few generations.

But perhaps you question all this reference back to the children of Israel in the wilderness. "Really now, has it any relevance to us, today?" some have asked.

In answer, I remind you of a passage in 1 Corinthians. Paul, indeed, recognized a wilderness stage in the Christian experience and made direct application, just as we have done:

> But with many of them God was not well pleased: for they were overthrown in the wilderness. Now these things were our examples, to the intent we should not lust after evil things, as they also lusted. Neither be ye idolaters, as were some of them; as it is written, The people sat down to eat and drink, and rose up to play. Neither let us commit fornication, as some of them committed, and fell in one day three and twenty thousand. Neither let us tempt Christ, as some of them also tempted, and were destroyed of serpents. Neither murmur ye, as some of them also murmured, and were destroyed of the destroyer. Now all these things happened unto them for ensamples: and they are written for our admonition, upon whom the ends of the world are come. Wherefore let him that thinketh he standeth take heed lest he fall (1 Cor. 10:5:12).

What about you? Have you recognized many of these characteristics within your own life? Are you one of those who tell how Jesus meets your needs rather than praising him for all your abundance?

Be honest! How big is your faith? Are you constantly up and down in your Christian experience? Do you possess more than a three-day faith? Do you know God is yours, or do you always need signs? Are you believing God for things to happen, or do you believe God only *if* things happen? How many things are you believing God for right now?

Is there anything you place before God: your job, your home, your golf, your car, your hobby, your boy friend? Are you holding out an idol or two? Do you have a secret besetting sin?

Are you a frequent complainer? Do you discourage easily? Do you find yourself longing to live like the ungodly? Do you long for the material things of the world . . . and find yourself living for that which can be enjoyed right now?

Are you quick to criticize your brother? Do you speak well of others, or do you catch yourself putting them down? Are you afraid to trust the Lord and believe him to fulfill all his promises?

Do many of these things characterize your experience? If so, you dwell in the wilderness and face the danger of never getting out. Don't stay too long in the wilderness.

It is still my conviction that most of the people we consider the best Christians in our church receive their mail in the wilderness. Some have moved in and out of the Promised Land. Most have never made it in. I do not say this to put them down but to lead them in!

With a sense of finality, the curtain closes like judgment falling upon Moses and his generation. They failed to make it through the wilderness.

ACT 3
Canaan
Conquest

Scene 10
How Will I Know When
I Have Arrived
"Wealth"

The curtain is drawn up for you to accompany the next generation of Israelites as they finally make it out of the wilderness. This time you approach Canaan from the east. The desert is left behind, as your caravan rises gradually on the plateau of Moab to a great ridge, about two miles long and one-half mile broad. With abruptness, the ridge drops 2,600 ft. down to the Jordan Valley. There it is! Before you lies the Promised Land. It stretches out in front of you like a wide green ribbon, between the ridge and the Mediterranean Sea. The view is breathtaking. The land is a wealth of agricultural productivity, a startling contrast to the desert wastelands. There is certainly no doubt that you have arrived!

I was speaking in Port Arthur, Texas, when a pastor requested a sermon on "spiritual geography." Seeing I was puz-

zled at the nature of this request, he explained: "My people
and I have been thinking about our spiritual condition. We
want you to teach on spiritual geography that we might know
just where we are, in our progress toward spiritual fullness."
In light of this need, we have already seen the characteristics of
Egypt, Chap. 2), and the wilderness (Chap. 9). Now let us
see the distinguishing landmarks of the Promised Land.

The book of Joshua sets forth a clear, beautiful view of the
conditions of God's children in Canaan. Use it as a test against
your life, and you can tell if you have reached your spiritual
Promised Land. Please note, the underlying method of this
test will be to examine the condition of God's children in the
Promised Land in contrast to their condition in the wilderness.

The Promised Land represents a mature, balanced spiritual
life, a life which enjoys the fullness of God's blessings. You
can know when you have arrived by testing your life for a
wealth of blessing and a wealth of belief.

A Wealth of Blessing

God met the needs of the children of Israel while they wandered in the wilderness. God provided guidance, food, and
clothing. He performed some miracles on their behalf. But for
those in the Promised Land, God does far more than merely
meet their needs, as precious as that is. Canaan is characterised by bounty:

For the Lord thy God bringeth thee into a good land, a land of
brooks of water, of fountains and depths that spring out of valleys
and hills; a land of wheat, and barley, and vines, and fig trees,
and pomegranates; a land of oil olive, and honey; a land wherein
thou shalt eat bread without scarceness, thou shalt not lack any
thing in it . . . when thy herds and thy flocks multiply, and thy
silver and thy gold is multiplied, and all that thou hast is multiplied (Deut. 8:7-9,13).

God gave them a land of multiplied blessings!

To enter the Promised Land, is to enter into the fullness of your earthly spiritual inheritance. Your weeks will begin to abound with blessings of various and sundry proportions. Whereas God has miraculously delivered you from difficulties in the past, now miracles will become more of a daily event, especially as God uses you on behalf of others. You will begin to experience a deep, lasting satisfaction and contentment in life.

In Egypt, the spiritual life is a series of defeats, interspersed with an occasional victory. In the wilderness your life vacillates; you are up for a while, then you are down. But in the Promised Land your life is characterised by a series of victories, interrupted only by occasional defeat. Your life will attain a level of consistant joy and peace. God will finally "put it all together" for you.

This is certainly not to imply that your life will be void of conflict. Your life will be tested, even in the Promised Land. There will be those "trying times." If for no other purpose, trials are necessary to keep you humble (Deut. 8:2). Moreover, one blessing of the Promised Land is the victory you enjoy in surmounting the conflict you encounter there. You finally learn why Paul could say, "Now thanks be to God, which always causeth us to triumph in Christ" (2 Cor. 2:14). Canaan represents a stage of spiritual development where all the exhilarating spiritual experiences that became yours through self-crucifixion and the filling of the Spirit, now become your constant manner of life!

But all this awaits your arrival in the Promised Land. There really is such a place. That is, there is an advanced stage of spiritual development to which you should aspire. The Bible speaks of "growing up" to a state of spiritual *maturity*. That's what Paul is speaking of when he encourages you to develop into "a *perfect* man, unto the measure of the statue of the *fulness* of Christ: that we henceforth be no more children . . . but . . . may grow up" (Eph. 4:14-15, italics added).

The Greek word here translated *perfect* is *teleioi*. It means perfect in the sense of mature. William Barclay says the word has reference to a person who is "full grown" in his personal development. Other translations render similar interpretations of the word perfect in this verse: "unto a fullgrown man" (ASV); "And to mature manhood and the stature of full-grown men in Christ" (Weymouth); "And reach the stature of manhood, and be of ripe age to receive the fullness of Christ" (Conybeare).

Note the phrase "fullness of Christ." You will never begin to enjoy the fullness of his divine life until you reach a speci-fied stage of spiritual development. This is a definite point in time, differing in the life of each one of us, when we become "full grown" spiritually. Some never make it. There are fre-quent biblical enjoinders not to remain a "baby" Christian (1 Cor. 3:1; Heb. 5:13). Your "journey into fullness" is a very real and necessary spiritual experience. The fullness of God's blessings await your attainment of spiritual maturity . . . then you can be trusted with the fullness of your inheritance, to enjoy throughout the rest of your life.

You attain this spiritual state, then continue on in it. Just as in your physical development, you progress through childhood and adolescence to a state of maturity, then you function as an adult. Correspondingly, the scripture urges you: to "become full-grown in the Lord — yes, to the point of being filled full with Christ. Then we will no longer be like children", but "become more and more in every way like Christ" (Eph. 4: 13-15; TLB).

To know when you have arrived simply take the "Praise Test." In the Promised Land you enjoy such many-splendored blessings you simply must praise God. There are no silent folks in Canaan! Life there is so good you have to tell about it. In fact a common pitfall of the Promised Land is to begin praising God so much that the phrase itself becomes habitual, a mere cliché. It does not glorify God to say "praise God" mechani-cally, meaninglessly, with every breath. But you will find rea-son to praise him constantly, out of heartfelt gratification, in your continual conquest of Canaan.

However, the Promised Land is not commensurate with the second blessing, if, by that term you refer to a second work of grace which is wrought upon the soul, apart from but equal in effect to regeneration. The Promised Land does not refer to a second experience apart from regeneration, nor one equal to regeneration, but it should be the outcome of regeneration.

Neither does the Promised Land refer to sinless perfection, which seems to have derived from John Wesley's term "Christian perfection." Some use this term in reference to a crisis experience of sanctification in which the old nature is eradicated and one attains a sinless state of perfection. To the contrary, Joshua and the children of Israel never did succeed in expelling the Jebusites from the Promised Land. They "could not drive them out: but the Jebusites dwell with the children of Judah at Jerusalem unto their day" (Josh. 15:63). Neither will your old nature be eradicated in this life. Even in the Promised Land, your old nature will ever reassert it's influence and necessitate constant pruning.

Urging constant watchcare against the old nature, one has said: "The Jebusite dwells within your borders whether you like it or not; he can be subdued but not exterminated. In view of this great danger, I can only advise you to watch yourself most carefully and to cut away all offending growths as soon as they appear."

A Wealth of Belief

The Promised Land is occupied by those who have a great deal of faith. It's inhabitants are quite divergent except they have this one trait in common, they exhibit much faith in God. After all, that is the way they got there, by exercising great faith.

The key to spiritual maturity and your full inheritance is the enlargement of your faith. P. T. Forsyth in *Christian Perfection* agrees: "Faith is the condition of spiritual maturity in the sense of adulthood, of entering on the real heritage of the soul. It is the soul coming to itself, coming of age, feeling its feet, entering on its native powers."[1]

Moses failed to lead his generation into the Promised Land because of their unbelief. In the last chapter we looked at seven characteristics of their lack of faith. The faith of those who enter the Promised Land will stand out in direct contrast to those seven deficiencies. You may check the adequacy of your faith by checking these seven areas.

(1) Test your virtue. In the wilderness Israel's goodness was up and down. When they entered Canaan they had developed virtue. That is, goodness became the natural and consistent expressions of their life: "And they answered Joshua, saying, all that thou commandest us we will do, and withersoever thou sendest us, we will go" (Josh. 1:16). The question is: "Are you doing every single thing you know you should do as a Christian"? Search your heart about this matter! For a mature Christian has enough faith to trust God, and obey in everything. That is why, "Abraham trusted God, and when God told him to leave home and go far away to another land which he promised to give him, Abraham obeyed" (Heb. 11:8, TLB).

(2) Test your knowledge. The Israelites tempted God in the wilderness saying, "Is the Lord among us or not" (Ex. 17:7). They were notorious sign seekers. But the next generation had such faith they not only knew God was with them, they knew God had given them the Promised Land even before they possessed it: "Truly the Lord hath delivered into our hands all the land" (Josh. 2:24).

The question is: "Are you right now believing God for miracles that you know will happen, even before they do?" What about it? Great faith *knows* God will come through (Mark 11:23-24). Such knowledge is the hallmark of real faith: "What is faith? It is the confident assurance that something we want is going to happen" (Heb. 11:1, TLB).

(3) Test your temperance. One characteristic of the Israelites in the wilderness was they kept an idol or two (Ex. 32:8). But the Israelites who entered the Promised Land were temperate. They were willing to wholly set themselves apart from idols and anything else in order to be used of God: "And Joshua said unto the people, Sanctify yourselves: for tomorrow

the Lord will do wonders among you" (Josh. 3:5). The question is: "Is there anything you are unwilling to give up for your Lord?" A real disciple will throw everything down to follow Jesus, just as the apostles dropped their nets. Great faith knows to "seek ye first the kingdom of God, and his righteousness; and all these things shall be added unto you" (Matt. 6:33).

(4) Test your patience. The children of Israel were forever complaining and murmuring in the wilderness (Ex. 15:22,24). They lived "beneath" their circumstances. They discouraged easily. But the generation that took the Promised Land had enough faith to quietly and persistently stay under the load and lift until the victory comes. That's called patience. Patience was the key to their taking Jericho:

And the Lord said unto Joshua, See, I have given into thine hand Jericho . . . and ye shall compass the city, all ye men of war, and go around about the city once. Thus shalt thou do six days . . . and the seventh day ye shall compass the city seven times, and the priests shall blow the trumpets (Josh. 6:2-4).

Little did they understand it, but they had enough faith to patiently obey. Joshua rose early each day and led his army around Jericho and back. For six days he did the same thing, just as God instructed. On the seventh day he circled the city seven times. Then they blew the trumpet. The great walls of the city crumbled and fell; victory was theirs! They joined the ranks of those who, like Abraham, "through faith and patience inherit the promises" (Heb. 6:12).

The question is: "Will you refuse to quit and stay under the load, serving God without complaint, no matter what?"

(5) Test your godliness. While in the wilderness the children of Israel often "fell a lusting" after things of the world (Num. 11:4). They "lusted exceedingly in the wilderness" (Ps. 106:14). However, in Canaan, they refused to countenance even one man who coveted worldly things and took them. The man "saw among the spoils a goodly Babylonish garment, and two hundred shekels of silver, and a wedge of gold of fifty shekels weight, *then I coveted them,* and took

them" (Josh. 7:21, italics added).

The question is: "Do you often covet the things of this world?" Be deeply honest. The man who makes the Promised Land must break every hold the world has upon his life. He will believe there is more to life than material things to be enjoyed here and now. He will have the faith to live for things of eternal value: "And this is the victory that overcometh the world, even our faith" (1 John 5:4).

(6) Test your brotherly kindness. In the wilderness the children of Israel were envious and judgemental (Num. 12:1-2). But in the Promised Land the children of Israel had developed brotherly love and kindness. An outstanding example of this was the attitude of Joseph's children when all the Promised Land was divided up among the tribes. They approached Joshua, who parceled out the land, to say: "Why have you given us only one portion of land when the Lord has given us such large populations" (Josh. 17:14, TLB). Take note, they didn't complain about what others were getting! When Joshua failed to respond as they had hoped (17:15), they asked again, stating simply: "The land is not enough for us" (17:16). They failed to get all they wanted, but never did they display envy at what others were receiving. Brotherly love prevailed!

The question is: "Do you love your brother enough not to be envious of him in any way?" I am indebted to Francis A. Schaeffer for that question. He says about the question, "Do not speak too quickly and say it is never so, because you will make yourself a liar."[2] He contends the greatest test of brotherly love is to check yourself for envy. Do you ever receive secret satisfaction at another man's misfortune? Do you ever find yourself disliking a person because you have a wrong desire toward something of his? The Israelites envied Moses and Aaron in the wilderness (Ps. 106:16). But great men of faith have such belief in their own significance before God that they rise above all envy (of any significance). It is always "the Jews which believed not" who are "moved with envy" (Acts 17:5).

(7) Test your love. The children of Israel were afraid to enter the Promised Land. But the next generation seemed to have no problem with fear at all, marching into battle after battle without the slightest hesitation. You see, they took seriously the first instruction for taking the land: "Hear therefore, O Israel, and observe to do it; that it might be well with thee, and that ye may increase mightily . . . in the land that floweth with milk and honey . . . *thou shalt love the Lord thy God with all thine heart*" (Deut. 6:3, 5, italics added). This generation of Israelites loved God with all their heart, and "perfect love casteth out fear" (1 John 4:18).

Francis A. Schaeffer has suggested an excellent, incisive test to determine whether you love God with all your heart. The question is: "Do you love God enough to be contented?"[3] And you are not truly content until you can thank God for everything! Schaeffer says that a quiet disposition and a heart giving thanks at any given moment is the real test of the extent to which we love God at that moment." Do you thank God in all the ebb and flow of life? Great faith loves God that much. It is content. Great faith believes in a personal universe and in a God of love. It believes enough to trust him. Great faith loves God contentedly, with a contentment of bountiful thanksgiving, "established in the faith . . . abounding therein with thanksgiving" (Col. 2:7).

As you read of Israel's conquest of Canaan, one thing that absolutely astonishes you is what is not said! Six chapters of Joshua are given over to a description of Israel in warfare (Ch. 6-11). This was followed by eleven chapters which records how the Promised Land was divided among them (Ch. 12-22). But in all the requirements of battle, and in the division of all their inheritance, the children of Israel never expressed discontent!

Let me summarize. The children of Israel developed in their faith before entering Canaan:

(1) from vacillation to virtue,
(2) from uncertainty to knowledge,
(3) from keeping an idol to temperance,

(4) from complaining to patience,
(5) from worldliness to godliness,
(6) from envious judging to brotherly kindness,
(7) from fearfulness to love.

And when you have enlarged your faith in these seven areas you will know you have spiritually "arrived" in the Promised Land. Spiritual maturity is, in itself, the attainment of a wealth of belief!

However, someone might say, "But doesn't this place undue significance on some Old Testament characteristics of faith?" Not at all! In his second epistle, Peter designates precisely these same qualities of faith as prerequisites for spiritual fullness. Since we have "like precious faith," he says you must "give all diligence" to exercise your faith to develop: virtue, knowledge, temperance, patience, godliness, brotherly kindness, love (2 Pet. 1:1-7).

As the curtain brings an end to this enjoyable scene, as if on a magic carpet, you are swept back by Canaan for a panoramic view of the Promised Land for one last look at the belief of those who made it there and the bounty that was theirs. Surely, the closing of the curtain will leave you with one thought, When I have attained such a wealth of belief, and such a wealth of blessing, I will know I have arrived!

Notes

1. P. T. Forsyth, *Christian Perfection* (London: Hodder & Stoughton), p. 103.

2. Francis A. Schaeffer, *True Spirituality* (Wheaton: Tyndale House Publishers, 1972), p. 13.

3. *Ibid.,* p. 9.

Scene 11
How to Take the Land
"Walking"

In the last scene you were taken on a tour of the Promised Land, with a view of examining its wealth.

As the curtain opens, Canaan comes into view again, but this time you see it from another angle. Now you view it from the perspective of its conquest. Seen from this point of view, it looks like one big warfare!

The Promised Land is enemy infested. Seven mighty nations occupy the land: The Hittites, the Amorites, the Girgashites, the Perizzites, the Hivites, the Jebusites, the Canaanites. Each and every one of them is "greater and mightier" than Israel (Deut. 7:1).

These enemy nations have walled cities replete with towers, huge gates, and citadels. They are fortified strongholds with massive arsenals of bows and arrows, swords, and daggers plus special weapons like the steel-edged Canaanite battle-axe. They have chariots of iron! The people of Canaan are tall and strong; their warriors renowned (Deut. 1:28).

How then, will Israel take the land?

Well, you won't believe the instruction they received! The book of Joshua opens with it. Their success in taking the land was based upon . . . their walk. "Moses my servant is dead; now therefore arise, go over this Jordan, thou, and all this people, unto the land which I do give to them, even to the children of Israel. Every place that the sole of your foot shall tread upon, that have I given you" (Josh. 1:2-3). They were limited only by the ground they covered.

Likewise, the New Testament speaks of a "walk in the Spirit" that guarantees victory over the flesh: "Walk in the Spirit, and

ye shall not fulfil the lust of the flesh" (Gal. 5:16). You are
limited only by your walk!

This brings us back to the basic premise of this book: fulfillment of the quest for spiritual fullness is found in the
journey itself, not in one final experience. The Christian walk
is not only the way into God's fullness, it is the experience.
When you finally reach the plateau of spiritual maturity and
continue on, you journey on the higher planes of a Promised
Land that satisfies!

The wilderness was characterised by wandering. As John
Hunter states, "Walking isn't wandering, walking is making
progress." The continual progress of your journey on in the
Promised Land is God's perfect will for your life.

The Way to Walk

Consider what God actually said. The whole land was given
to the children of Israel, but they could possess only the portion
they appropriated: "Every place that the sole of your foot shall
tread upon, that have I given you."

It was an enemy-infested land. Therefore, God promised to
give the Israelites all they had faith to walk through. Though
troubled on every side, they were not to turn "from the right
hand or to the left, that thou mayest prosper withersoever thou
goest" (Josh. 1:7).

You see, the spiritual life is a walk of faith (2 Cor. 5:7).
You must simply exercise faith to place one foot before the
other and continue on, trusting God for everything. You can
have all of God you have faith to appropriate, and the more you
appropriate, the more faith enlarges. You simply walk, taking
each step in dependence upon him, appropriating his strength
—one step at a time!

Such a walk gives glorious validity to one gigantic truth. It
is this: The Christian life can be lived. In that one measured
sentence, I have stated the most startling discovery of my
salvation. Oh, for years I questioned it. I still need to be constantly reminded of it. But I do at last believe it. The Christian
life can be lived!

This is headline news in our day. For ours is an age of spiritual drop-outs. The Baptists dry-out; the Roman Catholics rust-out; the Fundamentalists fall-out; the Ecumenicals cop-out; the Pentecostals blow-out; our youth trip-out; our workers wear-out; our crusade converts cut-out; and our old soldiers of the cross — they just fade-away!

However, I believe the one clear rally cry to regroup our forces would be this glorious reaffirmation: The Christian life can be lived!

However, it must also be said that the Christian life cannot be lived by just everybody. Nor just anybody. But only by the one great somebody, Jesus Christ our Lord. That's the secret of a spiritual life. The Christian life can be lived, but only by Christ.

You must have the right one living it! Opinion is down on the Christian life today. But there is nothing wrong with the Christian life if you have the right person living it. The Christian life can be lived by Christ! It is exclusively his to live. He designed it to be lived. He assigned it to be lived. But only by himself.

That's why the Christian life is so difficult. You are forever trying to live it in your own strength when it can only be lived in dependence upon him. This is the sum and substance of the spiritual way of life. It is an exchanged life. You exchange your life for Christ's, that he might live his life in you. "I am crucified with Christ: nevertheless I live; yet not I but Christ liveth in me" (Gal. 2:20).

That's it. Indwelt and infilled, your life can pulsate with the living wonder of the Son of God as you appropriate his life for your own. It is a spiritual law: Every demand upon your life is a demand upon the Christ within you. By faith, you appropriate him.

I have been a minister of the gospel for twenty years. I have never found myself adequate for anything. My life is an endless exercise of faith in appropriating all Christ is for all he desires of me. I appropriate his love for caring, his patience for enduring, his wisdom for understanding, his calm for not retaliating. I simply draw endlessly from the well which never can run dry!

The principle of appropriation is simple: The more I appropriate of him, the less I live in the flesh (Gal. 5:16). This places the emphasis of your life on the positive rather than the negative.

During autumn the leaves begin to fall as winter comes. Some leaves fall later, as the winter winds blow. But some tenaciously hold on, dead and ugly. There are two ways to get those remaining leaves off the trees. You can knock them off by beating them with a stick. Or you can wait until the summer comes and the sun warms up everything. Then new life-sap comes up in the tree, and dead leaves fall to earth. God doesn't take a stick to your life and hurriedly rush at you to knock off all your dead leaves and fruits. You lose them little by little. He takes you on through to a springtime experience in which the life of his Son can flow through you, then that which is dead and ugly will drop away. Even in the Promised Land, God doesn't finish his work in a year. "I will not drive them out from before thee in one year . . . by little and little I will drive them out from before thee, until thou be increased, and inherit the land" (Ex. 23:29-30).

You receive the strength for your walk through some abiding pathways.

Abiding Pathways

In Alan Redpaths book on Joshua, he devotes three chapters to "encamping at Gilgal." The Scriptures state: "And the people came up out of Jordan on the tenth day of the first month, and *encamped in Gilgal* . . . and those twelve stones, which Joshua took out of Jordan, did Joshua pitch in Gilgal" (Josh. 4:19-20, italics added).

He reminds us that "Gilgal became holy ground to the people of Israel. Throughout this whole book of Joshua you will find that Gilgal was the base of their operations against the enemy. It was a place to which Joshua frequently returned in the midst of his battles . . . he found himself again and again *going back to Gilgal.*"[1] Joshua returned to Gilgal to renew his strength!

In the same way, you must learn to encamp in our Lord, to abide. Once you have arrived in the Promised Land, the way to stay is by abiding in Christ.

Jesus said: "Abide in me, and I in you. · As the branch cannot bear fruit of itself, except it abide in the vine; no more can ye, except ye abide in me. I am the vine, ye are the branches: He that abideth in me . . . the same bringeth forth much fruit: for without me ye can do nothing" (John 15:4-5).

This verse is often referred to. But I have read little which *adequately* tells us how to abide. May I point out the way? Abide means to remain, and you remain in Christ by returning again and again as the Jews returned to Gilgal. You beat a path through the ways in which you have come to know him: through faith, through the Scriptures, through a filling of the Spirit, through love, through prayer, through obedience, through cleansing, and through witnessing.

In the following illustration the dashes represent the paths, or means by which we came to know Christ.

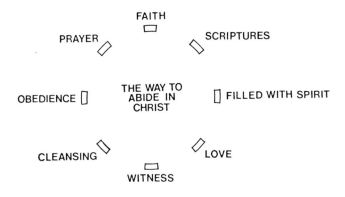

You abide in Christ by constantly returning over the paths by which you came to know him. See these as eight paths of spiritual exercise, through which you remain in Christ. All eight are vital. (1) You abide in Christ by maintaining your *faith* in him, believing him for all he wants to share of himself. (2) You communicate with him through the *Scriptures,* with which he speaks to you and (3) through *prayer,* by which you speak with him. (4) But it is the *Spirit* who reveals and imparts Jesus to you. (5) Furthermore, your experience together is a *love* relationship. (6) Also, your fellowship can be broken by sin. But if you confess your sin, you are *cleansed,* and fellowship is restored. (7) But your fellowship with Christ is never passive. You are yoked with him in service, which requires *obedience* on your part. (8) Yes, and you can't maintain full fellowship with him unless you are allowing him to *witness* of his life through you, which is the objective of it all!

As you faithfully exercise yourself along these eight paths, you receive the same kind of inner reinforcement the Israelites received by returning back to Gilgal. The secret is to exercise yourself in these areas simultaneously and consistently.

Paul cautions you about this. He begins his major treatise on spiritual warfare by stating: "Finally, my brethren, be *strong* in the Lord."

I saw something recently which epitomized the kind of inner strength Paul was referring to. While flying over the city of New Orleans, I got a glimpse of their magnificent domed stadium under construction. I had read a great deal about the new stadium and was peering out the window of my plane, hopeful of a good aerial view of it. I saw it but was disappointed, at first. They were just completing the superstructure in the great roof. From the air, all I saw looked like this:

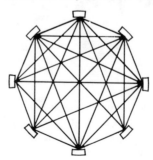

But as the plane flew on, my mind began to dwell upon what I had seen. Suddenly the thought struck me, A strong spiritual life should look like that. I mean, looking down from heaven's perspective, God must long to see such superstructure within your life. You must be strengthened within, to withstand the outside pressures of the world around you.

It takes a daily walk down the paths I have mentioned. Continuance in all eight of these exercises is the way to inward strength. You see, each one of these eight functions strengthens and is strengthened by the other. Each contributes to the others. When each of them functions together, they produce a cohesive effect on the inward man.

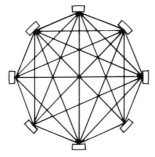

For sake of illustration, look within the circle of the visual analogy I used at the first of this discussion. Take faith as an example. Since it is a necessary ingredient for all the other exercises, draw a line within the circle from faith to each of the others to represent the buttressing effect faith has.

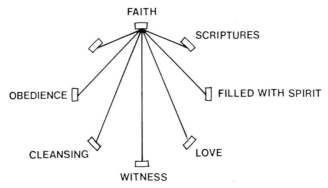

The lines within the circle illustrate the fact that faith is a necessary ingredient in all the other exercises:

The *Scriptures* must be received by faith (Heb. 4:2).

We receive the *spirit* by faith (Gal. 3:14).

We develop *love* from our faith (Eph. 3:17).

We get the spirit's power to *witness* by faith (Acts 1:8).

We *cleanse* our hearts by faith (Acts 15:9).

We *obey* our Lord by faith (Heb. 11:8).

Our *prayers* are assured by faith (Jas. 5:15).

But we can say the same of the Scriptures. They, too, are a necessary ingredient in all the other exercises:

The Scriptures are the sword of the *Spirit* (Eph. 6).

We are *spirit filled* on a scriptural promise (Acts 2:33).

The Scripture commands *love* (John 15:10,12).

We use the Scriptures in *witnessing* (Luke 8:11).

We are *clean* by the Word (Acts 15:3).

We are to *obey* the Word (2 Thes. 3:14).

We *pray* according to the Scriptures (Luke 11).

Faith comes from hearing the Word (Rom. 10:17).

So let us illustrate this, too, by a second line — from Scriptures to all the other exercises. Now our visual analogy looks something like this:

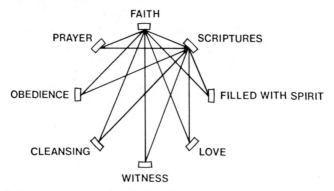

Going on around the circle of our visual analogy, the Holy Spirit is next. It also is a necessary ingredient in each of the other exercises:

Love is shed abroad by the Spirit (Rom. 5:5).
We best *witness* in the Spirit (Acts 4:31).
We are *cleansed* by the Spirit (1 Cor. 6:11).
We *obey* through the Spirit (Rom. 8:13).
We *pray* with the Spirit's help (Rom. 8:26).
Faith is the fruit of the Spirit (Gal. 5:22).
The *Scriptures* are revealed by the Spirit (1 Cor. 2:10,12).

Thus, when you add another line, from the Spirit to all the other exercises, our visual analogy takes on further inward structure but is a little one-sided.

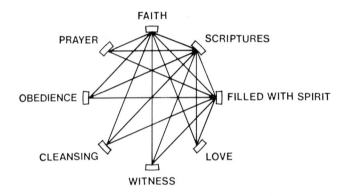

Surely, by now you see where we are headed. All eight of the activities contribute interchangeably. They relate reciprocally. Not one of them can be what it should be without the others. Not one fails to strengthen the others. When you grow slack in one, all the others will be weaker for it. On the other hand, for each one which actively functions, all the rest are strengthened. Faithfulness in all these areas is the way you fulfill Paul's command: "to be strengthened with might by his Spirit in the inner man . . . that ye might be filled with all the fulness of God" (Eph. 3:16,19).

You see, when we draw a line to represent each function as it contributes to the other, the visual analogy represents a balanced experience and looks like this:

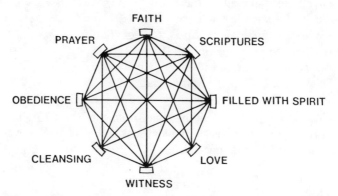

There is your picture of inward strength! How is that for inner structure? Satan will never crush a life with that kind of interlacing, internal support. You are equal to an onslaught of satanic attack! That's the way to prolong your days in the Promised Land. Strengthened with might in the inner man, you stay in!

As the curtain falls, a voice from off stage is heard to say: "Ye shall walk in all the ways which the Lord your God hath commanded you, that ye may live, and that it might be well with you, and that ye may prolong your days in the land which ye shall possess" (Deut. 5:33).

Now turn to the back of the book to the section in Spiritual Aids II entitled "For Strength." Fill it out very carefully. Commit yourself to consistent exercise in each and every pathway. Don't be legalistic about it! Don't get frustrated when you fail to be faithful. You will be spending the rest of your life seeking consistency. But begin now; and honestly, unceasingly press on. Your victory will equal your progress!

Notes

1. Alan Redpath, *Victorious Christian Living* (Old Tappan, N. J.: Fleming H. Revell Co., 1955), p. 66.

Scene 12
How to Conquer the Enemy
"Warfare"

Drums of war rumble in the background, as the curtain opens upon the armies of Israel gathered in solemn array. Leaders of the twelve tribes encircle a central fire within the camp. Fanning out from that fire in each direction is a vast sea of soldiers. It is a council of war!

All are seated but Joshua and two men who have just returned from a reconnaissance mission. They have scouted the enemy and are about to suggest a strategy of attack. Listen! For what you are about to hear is almost unheard of in the annals of warfare.

The two advance scouts address the council to make this report: "Truly the Lord hath delivered into our hands all the land; for even all the inhabitants of the country do faint because of us" (Josh. 2:24). The enemy is already defeated. Israel can go to battle in the strength of knowing the war is already won!

What seemed to be such a formidable foe is vanquished — the enemy has been as good as defeated since the day Moses crossed the Red Sea: "I know that the Lord hath given you the land. . . . For we have heard how the Lord dried up the water of the Red Sea for you, when ye came out of Egypt. . . . As soon as we had heard these things, our heart did melt, neither did there remain any more courage in any man" (Josh. 2:9-11).

Think of it! Had Moses' generation simply exercised faith, they *could* have taken the land. But they cringed before a defeated foe!

Let us transpose the journey of Israel into your spiritual journey at this point, for you, too, must prepare for battle. Indeed, the moment you enter the Promised Land, your conflict with Satan will intensify into out-and-out warfare.

The apostle Paul, speaking about this warfare, urged us to develop holding action. Every time you gain new ground in the Promised Land, Satan will counterattack. It will be all you can do to stand your ground. "Finally, my brethren, be strong in the Lord, and in the power of his might. Put on the whole armour of God, that ye may be able to stand against the wiles of the devil. . . . that ye may be able to withstand in the evil day, and having done all, to stand" (Eph. 6:10-11,13). Be prepared! Stand your ground! Learn the finer techniques of spiritual warfare!

The most vital information for combating Satan is the truth embodied in the scouts report to Joshua: the enemy is already defeated. This reveals the "battle strategy" from which you will wage your war. Unique in the annals of warfare, your spiritual battle strategy is this: You war from victory, not to it! You see, Satan is a defeated foe. In fact, one of the reasons Christ came to earth was to incapacitate the devil: "For this purpose the Son of God was manifested, that he might destroy the works of the devil" (1 John 3:8).

Having spoiled the principalities and powers of Satan, he made a show of them openly, triumphing over them at his cross (Col. 2:15). Jesus enjoyed total triumph. He resisted all temptation. God demonstrated his sovereignty over Satan by fashioning the cross into the instrument of this world's salvation. Having done this, he announced: "All authority is given me, in heaven and in earth" (Matt. 28:18, ASV). This same authority has been passed on to you (Luke 10:17-19). Because of this, you can battle with Satan from the authority of your position in the Lord. Satan has no power but what is allowed him. Think of it! If you leave him unchallenged, you rob Jesus of a portion of Calvary's triumph.

The exact action you are to take, in light of that strategy, is revealed in a concise statement by James: "Submit yourselves therefore to God. Resist the devil, and he will flee from you"

(Jas. 4:7). Now, you can determine your weapons on the basis of this action.

Offensive Weapons

Your offensive action is to: "Submit yourselves to God." Therefore, you need to gain proficiency in the following *two* offensive weapons:

Yield to your Savior. The first step in dealing with the devil is to yield your life to Jesus. Remember our discussion in chapter 4. Yielding is not a passive experience. To yield is to report for duty. To yield is to obey each divine impulse. Do all he asks in his strength. You exchange your life for his that he might express his great life through you. Determine to be the kind of man of whom it is said, "Christ is seen to live again."

Then when Satan knocks at your door, let Jesus answer! Jesus can handle him: "Greater is he that is in you [Jesus], than he that is in the world [Satan]" (1 John 4:4).

Die to yourself. Don't forget your self-centered old nature. Else you will yield your life only to find yourself taking back what you yielded. You must not only yield to the Savior, but you must also die to yourself. Choose death to all self-centeredness, and trust the Holy Spirit to carry out the execution!

The vital point I wish to make here is for you to recognize the correlation of these two actions. They are exactly the same ones referred to by the apostle Paul in his great chapter on victory over sin. He mentions these two actions in Romans 6:11,13: "Reckon ye also yourselves dead indeed unto sin. . . . But yield yourselves unto God, as those that are alive from the dead, and your members as instruments of righteousness unto God."

There will never be a day, in the Promised Land, but that you will have need to yield yourself unto God, and reckon death to yourself in regard to the flesh and its sin. Paul said, "I die daily" (1 Cor. 15:31).

Dr. Stephen Olford is only too correct in his interpretation of Paul's further statement in Romans 12:1: "I beseech you therefore, brethren, by the mercies of God, that ye present your bodies a living sacrifice, holy, acceptable unto God, which is your reasonable service."

To present yourself "a living sacrifice" means to ever live sacrificially. Make your life one constant sacrifice. The Old Testament required burnt offerings. In this sacrifice the meat was placed on the altar and held in the flames until it was wholly consumed. Your sacrifice is similar, in that your life is to be totally submitted — forever! You are to live sacrificially.

A young lady came to Dr. Olford at the close of a service and said: "All this business about consecration and surrender is sheer nonsense. It simply does not work." To which he replied: "My friend, you have lied to God and to me, for I know you have never truly yielded your life." Rather shaken, she replied, "But I have." "But you have not," he insisted. "That is, you have not submitted in the New Testament sense. New Testament surrender is not a day, a week, a month, or a year. It is a contract for life. If you say you have surrendered your life to God, what are you doing off the altar?"[1]

Think of these weapons as two "fleshhooks." In the Old Testament God gave the children of Israel special instructions about burnt sacrifices. When they placed a sacrifice on an altar to be burned, the priest used two "fleshhooks" (Ex. 38: 3). With these, he would keep the sacrifice upon the altar and continue pulling it toward the center of the flame, until it was totally consumed.

You have two fleshhooks: yielding to your Savior and dying to yourself.

Use these two fleshhooks to keep yourself on the altar of sacrifice, totally and continually submitted unto God. These are your offensive weapons!

Defensive Weapons

Your defensive action is to: "Resist the devil, and he will flee from you." You see, I have said much in warning about Satan because most Christians entirely ignore him! That is what he counts on. But remember, he is a defeated foe. It is only through your ignorance of him that he will gain advantage of you (2 Cor. 2:11). When you acknowledge him to resist him, he must flee. You have authority over the devil (Luke 10:17-19). Resist him!

You have two defensive weapons. Resist him: by rejoicing and rejecting.

You resist by rejoicing. Let's get it all together by reviewing what we have previously learned about the testing process and add our new truth! Examine the following illustration:

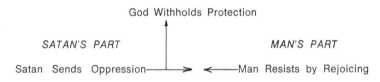

GOD'S PART

God Withholds Protection

SATAN'S PART   *MAN'S PART*

Satan Sends Oppression—————> <————Man Resists by Rejoicing

Here is the explanation:

Satan sends oppression toward us (arrow from left to right).

God will prevent it or allow it (arrow going up).

But man can resist by rejoicing (arrow right to left).

As we have stated, one method of satanic attack is to oppress you. But you can resist the oppressions of the devil. You are not defenseless. Even if God allows him to send some affliction upon you, God will always work it out to your good (Rom. 8:28). Your part is to resist, by refusing to let it get you down! Believe God to make a blessing out of it!

Whom resist stedfast in the faith, knowing that the same afflictions are accomplished in your brethren that are in the world. But the God of all grace, who hath called us unto his eternal glory by Christ Jesus, after that ye have suffered a while, make you perfect, stablish, strengthen, settle you (1 Peter 5:9, 10).

You can resist the devil's attempt to oppress you, and the way to resist his oppressions is by rejoicing.

How well I remember when I first learned this truth. A

minister friend had stopped by my study to see me. In the course of our conversation, I was sharing the circumstances of a trial I was passing through. He seemed to understand and offered encouragement. But when he arose to leave, he paused at the door, turned, and made one parting statement that exploded in my heart: "But you know, Jim, we never really have the victory in these times until we can come to the place where we rejoice and praise God for the situation!"

It stunned me! My heart sank in shame at my complaining. That very day I had read something similar somewhere in the Scriptures. I picked up my Bible to search for it and finally found the passage. This time its truth took hold of me: "Wherein ye greatly rejoice, through now for a season, if need be, ye are in heaviness through manifold temptation [trials]: that the trial of your faith . . . might be found unto praise and honor and glory at the appearing of Jesus Christ" (1 Pet. 1:6,7).

You must prepare yourself for such trials. Expect them; be ready for them; thank God through them. "Beloved, think it not strange concerning the fiery trial which is to try you, as though some strange thing happened unto you: but rejoice" (1 Pet. 4:12,13).

Never forget, the objective of satanic oppression is discouragement. The one most noticeable thing about the children of Israel in the wilderness was their unceasing tendency to murmur and complain at every trial.

I, too, experience those times when I blindly stumble into a web of satanic circumstance. Sometimes it has been severe enough to have stripped me bare of everything I held dear in my life. These are desperate times — fearful and excruciating trials. But I am learning to ignore all circumstances. I refuse to accept them as final, get a tenacious grip on God's grace, and hold on with all my faith until I can rejoice in the situation. Then God comes through! He always does!

Satan is bound when you can rejoice through every oppression!

You resist by rejecting. Let's get it all in perspective again by recalling the rest of our testing process and applying one more truth. Adding to the previous illustration, we get it all together:

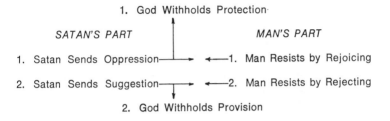

GOD'S PART

1. God Withholds Protection

SATAN'S PART   *MAN'S PART*

1. Satan Sends Oppression ————→ ←—— 1. Man Resists by Rejoicing

2. Satan Sends Suggestion ————→ ←—— 2. Man Resists by Rejecting

2. God Withholds Provision

Here is the explanation of the lower portion:

> Satan comes with suggestions (arrow from left to right),
> God sometimes withholds some provision of your daily needs (arrow down),
> But man can resist by rejecting his suggestions (arrow right to left).

God gave me a great discovery concerning how to resist the devil. Once I did a word study on the phrase, "resist the devil and he will flee from you." I was asking myself, "Just how are we to resist?" What does resist mean?

The word "resist" is translated from the Greek word *anthistemi*. It means to reject. I found the very same word is used in Ephesians where we are told to put on the whole armor of God that we may be able to stand against the wiles of the devil. But the word *anthistemi* is here translated "withstand." The actual verse says, "Wherefore take unto you the whole armor of God, that ye may be able to *anthistemi* [withstand or resist] in the evil day, and having done all, to stand" (Eph. 6:13, italics added).

This verse reveals you are to *anthistemi* (resist) the devil by putting on the whole armor of God!

The passage in Ephesians describes that armor in detail. You are to take: (1) a belt of *truth;* (2) a breastplate of *righteousness;* (3) sandals of *peace;* (4) a shield of *faith,*

(5) a helmet of salvation, which is a helmet of *hope* (1 Thes. 5:8); (6) and our sword is the *Word*.

But what does this really mean? Where do you obtain this armor?

The answer to that is still most simple. As Christians, you already have all these qualities within you, in the person of the indwelling Christ. You appropriate them from him. You put on Christ (Rom. 13:14). (1) Christ is your truth (John 14:6). (2) Christ is your righteousness (1 Cor. 1:30). (3) Christ is your peace (John 16:33). (4) Christ is your faith (Heb. 12:2). (5) Christ is your hope (1 Tim. 1:1). (6) and Christ is the Word (John 1:1).

Furthermore, the passage in Ephesians tells you *how* to put on the armor. You appropriate it through prayer: "Praying always with all prayer and supplication in the Spirit, and watching thereunto" (Eph. 6:18).

Do you see it? The way to reject satan's suggestions is to tell Jesus on him! That is, you go to Jesus in prayer and appropriate what you need of him to reject all of the devil's suggestions. The armor of Ephesians is enough to turn back every suggestion of Satan.

Let me be explicit.

(1) Satan will come with suggestions of deceit, to "fill thine heart to lie," as the Bible teaches (Acts 5:3).

Ask Jesus to be your truth, and keep you truthful (2 *Thess. 2:10*).

(2) Satan the accuser will come with suggestions which degrade you and stir up false guilt (1 Tim. 5:15, Rev. 12:10).

Ask Jesus to be your righteousness and trust your acceptance with God in him (*Phil. 3:9*).

(3) Satan will come with suggestions to distract your mind with wayside worries, as in Mark 4:15.

Ask Jesus to be your peace. Divine peace can calm the mind and rid it of anxiety and worry (*Phil. 4:7*)*!*

(4) Satan will come with suggestions of doubt as he did in Genesis 3:1-5.

Ask Jesus to be your shield of faith, dissolving every fiery dart of doubt (Luke 22:31,32).

(5) Satan will come with suggestions of defeat when he wins a battle, as in 1 Thessalonians 2:19.

Ask Jesus to be your hope, for though you might lose a battle, you will win the war (1 Tim. 1:1)!

(6) Satan will come with wicked suggestions of disobedience, as in Mark 4:15.

Ask Jesus to remind you of his Word, reject all illegitimate desire and turn back the devil with a refusal and a rebuke (Matt. 4:3-11).

Be consistent! When you repeat an act often enough, it becomes a habit. Reject Satan in this manner often enough and it will become habitual for you to go to Jesus at every testing. These six responses will become second nature with you — appropriating Christ as your truth, your righteousness, your peace, your faith, your hope and your discipline. It will become a natural reflex to respond with that of Christ which turns Satan away!

The key to this is to reject temptation immediately! When Satan suggests some evil deed, do not let your mind dwell on it. Do not consider the prospect of it. By all means, do not begin to contemplate the situation in the imagination of your mind. These thoughts have a way of lingering within the mind. They make you more susceptible to similar thoughts later. Each repeated thought will weaken your resistance. Think about something long enough, and you are likely to do it. "As [a man] thinketh in his heart, so is he" (Prov. 23:7).

In my travels I have found it a common practice in some quarters to emphasize a further method of rejecting Satan. Some not only reject his suggestions, but they vocally dismiss him from their presence. Indeed, Jesus addressed Satan vocally and ordered him away (Matt. 4:10; Mark 8:33).

These are your weapons for satanic conflict. Offensively, you submit: yielding to your Savior and dying to yourself. Defensively, you resist: rejoicing through oppression and rejecting his suggestions.

In conclusion, may I remind you that Jesus, after having been filled with the spirit was led into the wilderness to be tried by the devil (Luke 4:1). For forty days he was oppressed in a wilderness setting, thirsting for food and drink, but he faithfully trusted through it. Then Satan came at him with subtle suggestion, but Jesus rejected the devil with Scripture. Jesus accomplished in forty days what the children of Israel had not accomplished in forty years! Furthermore, he was equally victorious throughout his life. On the night before the cross, he said, "The prince of this world cometh, and hath nothing in me."

As we previously mentioned, "no man can enter into a strong man's house, and spoil his goods, except he will first bind the strong man; and then he will spoil his house" (Mark 3:27). But the strong man (Satan) is bound when there is nothing in you that responds!

As the curtain descends to end this scene, you are caught away, only to reappear alone on the stage. It is seven years later, and you are standing before a large plaque in the palace of Palestine. The plaque commemorates the victory of Joshua over the enemy. It reads: "So Joshua conquered the entire land — the hill country, the Negeb, the land of Goshen, the lowlands, the Arabah, and the hills and lowlands of Israel," and, "Joshua took the entire land just as the Lord had instructed Moses; and he gave it to the people of Israel as their inheritance" (Josh. 11:16,23, TLB). Hallelujah!

Turn back again to the end of this book, and read the Spiritual Aid II entitled "Declaration of War." Refer to it constantly, until you habitually defeat the devil! The Promised Land demands your preparedness for battle!

Notes

1. Stephen F. Olford, *I'll Take the High Road* (Grand Rapids: Zondervan Publishing House, 1969), p. 31.

Scene 13
The Journey's End
"Witnessing"

The curtain lifts to present our final scene. The setting is simple, the occasion momentous. The tribes of Reuben, Gad, and Manasseh have gathered on the Jordan border. The purpose of their gathering is to erect a "great altar" to God (Josh. 22:10).

The princes of Israel were greatly pleased with the altar, because it was erected as a witness of God to following generations (Josh. 22:27). The altar was to "be a witness between us that the Lord is God" (Josh. 22:34). They called it "The Altar of Witness" (TLB).

There is one spiritual activity which supersedes all others in importance. When it receives proper emphasis, the others have a way of falling in place. If it is lacking, God will withdraw the fullness of his power! I speak of God's witness through your life! It is, by the way, God's witness. It isn't your witness so much as it is his. He gives expression of his life through you. Perhaps the major problem in modern evangelism is an inadequate concept which says, "We are to witness for him!" We are not to witness for him, so much as we are to witness of him. And we only do this by learning to witness with such dependence on his Spirit that he is witnessing of himself through us.

This is your journey's end. Witnessing is the goal — the objective — of your journey. It is the ultimate purpose of your life.

Think with me! You are on a "journey into fullness." But, when you reach that fullness, what will you be full of? Peter tells us: "Whereby are given unto us exceeding great and precious promises: that by these ye might be partakers of the divine nature" (2 Pet. 1:4). God wants to fill you with his divine nature. That was God's plan from the beginning. You are predestined "to be conformed to the image of his Son" (Rom. 8:29). Your life is to be full of God.

The motive behind all God did for Israel was the witness of God through them (Ex. 16:7,12). That is his will today. He wants to express his life through you for a witness of himself in this godless world! And his image must be projected clearly. When other things crowd into the picture, you suffer double exposure and the image is blurred.

Therefore, along with the eight exercises spoken of in chapter 11, one other thing is imperative if you are to retain God's fullness. You must give attention to the focus of your life!

When I was a boy, my father represented the Lions Club in our small town and traveled to New York City to attend the World's Fair. I remember it like yesterday because he brought me back a tremendous souvenir, the kind only a dad would have thought of. It was my first magnifying glass. It was a powerful little thing. It folded up into its own little case, and it was "pocket" size. It had "New York World's Fair" written on it in gold letters, at first. But I carried it so long the gold wore off.

Even with the loss of this prestige, it was easily the classiest magnifying glass in my school room, and I treasured it. Its power was always a wonder to me. There were so many uses for a magnifying glass. It has never ceased to puzzle me how boys these days ever get along without one. How can they ever get a close look at bugs or read the small lettering on labels? I wonder how they magnify words to the fellow seated next to them in school or start fires without a match. The lessons of that glass are with me yet, and a few of them have contributed to my grasp of life itself. For example, I have always had a profound respect for focus.

You can take a magnifying glass and place it in between the sun and a piece of paper. The lens will draw several light rays to focus at a common point. Move it back and forth to get it properly focused until a tiny image of the sun is thrown on the paper. In a few moments, heat will ignite the paper, and it will burst into flame.

It is the same with your life. Move it in between the Son and a lost world. Then move your life back and forth until it is in proper focus, until a tiny image of the Son is projected through you to a point in this world. In time, the result is powerful and combustive! Having done all, you must give strict attention to the focus of your life!

Openness to the Son

The focus of your life depends upon openness to the Son. It naturally follows, then, that you must keep your life open to the full reflection of the Son through you! Indeed, the Bible seems to indicate the passing of his image through us is actually what transforms us into his likeness. Insert one word from modern translations, and we have this verse: "But we all, with open face [reflecting] as in a glass the glory of the Lord, are changed into the same image from glory to glory, even as by the Spirit of the Lord" (2 Cor. 3:18).

Do you realize what this means? If our lives close up to his witness through us, we cease to be changed! He only expresses his life in us by releasing it through us. It is a spiritual law: Our transformation will equal our transparency! We must, then, keep our journey's end in view — we are to be a witness.

The ultimate objective of a Spirit-filled life is to witness! The deepest desire in the heart of God, the deepest thought in the mind of God, the deepest action in the will of God is the expression of God in and through your life.

How can you claim to live in the Promised Land if the activity of your life is not centered in witnessing? Everybody living in God's country will be concerned with witnessing of him. They will have tried and failed, struggled and cried, trusted and won through until their lives begin to affect others! Richard Hogue caught this concept and placed it in a book on witnessing. His book, *The Jesus Touch,* is the first book I would want you to read as a sequel to this one. As he so aptly put it: Witnessing will become your "life-style." The person who is filled and controlled by the Holy Spirit will "witness as naturally as he puts on his pants in the morning . . . as naturally as a radio commentator gives the news . . . as naturally as a football player dons a helmet."

I say it with deep conviction: God will cease to fill any life that closes itself off from the world. God's life must pass through you. In the process you are changed, and others receive the witness of him.

Closeness to the Lost

The focus of your life depends upon closeness to the lost. One other thing about that magnifying glass: The magnifying power of its lens depends on its focal length. The focal length is the distance from the lens to the object. The average focal length of a magnifying glass is about ten inches.

Mark it down. Your life will never have much influence on those you know from afar. You will never be an effective witness if you keep everyone at arm's length. You must get close to people, about ten inches close! You must really get next to people for an effective witness. This will necessitate some buttonholing, very personal confrontations. You must verbally speak to people. Share with them face to face!

In years gone by, many who have been unwilling to give a spoken witness, have excused themselves by saying, "I witness by my life." Not to mention the fact that this smacks of unmitigated egotism, their witness is usually inadequate because such a person fails to get close to people. Such a witness is usually given from afar. Besides, if your life is, indeed, a good example, people will not likely know that Christ is the source of your strength unless you tell them. Otherwise, you get the glory!

Witnessing person to person requires closeness. You must be face to face. That is the proper focus. This activity is usually referred to as personal soul-winning.

Hold it! I could almost envision your reaching forward to turn me off at the mention of soul-winning. Most folks don't enjoy this emphasis. We all feel guilty about our neglect and unconcern. But let it be known that no man reaches the Promised Land without developing a personal concern for others. Moreover, once in the land, if not before, we inevitably share that concern by spoken expressions person to person. It is impossible to experience the blessings of the Promised Land and keep quiet about it! You *will* share. Jesus said it: "And ye shall be witnesses unto me." Not you *might* be, but you *will* be.

The Old Testament tells of a time when the Syrians besieged Samaria. They camped outside it until the Samaritans ran out of food. The famine was so desperate that babies were boiled and eaten (2 Kings 6). During the night the Lord made the Syrians to hear a sound like the thundering of horses' hooves, like a mighty host riding against them. They thought the Hittites or Egyptians had been summoned, so they panicked and fled their camp in the twilight, leaving all their possessions behind.

Four leprous beggars ventured out of famine-ridden Samaria and wandered into the Syrian camp. They found it deserted. The lepers shouted with joy and ran through the camp. They entered tents, ate their fill, spoiled the camp of all the goods they could carry, and then thought of their friends who were starving. Being men of principle, they said to one another: "This isn't right. This is wonderful news, and we aren't sharing it with anyone! . . . Come on, let's go back and tell the people" (2 Kings 7:9, TLB).

Those in the Promised Land have known an experience just like that. The Lord has taken care of the enemy; they have entered his camp, experienced what it is to be filled, and spoiled his goods. Inevitably they will respond: "This is wonderful news, and we aren't sharing it with anyone . . . come on, let's go back and tell the people" (2 Kings 7:9).

To the contrary, some Christians have entered the Promised Land, only to fall away from spiritual wealth because they never became witnesses. They refused to share their good news. God will withhold his richest blessings from such a man.

In summary, with all your doing, give special attention to the focus of your life. The focus of your life depends upon your openness to the Son. You must so relate your life to him that he might reflect his life through you to a point in this godless world. But the focus of your life also depends upon your closeness to people. Remember, proper focus length is ten inches — you must witness face to face!

As the last curtain falls upon these panoramic scenes of our "journey into fullness," I make this final plea with measured words. If I never write another book, if these are my last words, I want them to be a plea for redemptive action. I urge you to witness. Is it nothing to you that the masses know not our Lord? Jesus came "to seek and to save that which was lost" (Luke 19:10). What is the driving ambition of your life? Can you be saved and refuse to help rescue others? Can you be spiritually full and be unconcerned for those who are empty? Can you expect God to give your life his fullest attention if you ignore those in need of you? I think not! Excuses are unacceptable. If you seldom lead anyone to a saving knowledge of Jesus Christ, your life is less than what God expects!

There is a direction of life that leads to wonderful fullness, but you will reach a plateau of ecstacy only to slip away unless you share it all with others. The focused life is transparent, witnessing with a clear reflection of him so that others come to walk beside you along the way!

God deliver me from any spiritual emphasis that is nothing more than a glorified self-improvement course. God wants to get "alive" in this world. He would like to burst out through your life. But he does not intend to stop with you. He reaches through you to others. They, too, need his fullness. Oh, how God transforms the man who loses himself in total abandon, that others may know Christ!

TRAVELER'S AIDS I

For Use in Egypt   *Obituary Notice*

On _____ (Date), at _____ (Place),
having been crucified with Christ, I sign this obituary as mine.

_____ (Name)

Instructions for Daily Self-Destruction!

Pray in this manner:

1. "Lord, I confess the existence of this self-centered bent, this "old nature" within me. I recognize it as the source of all my sin.

2. I render a judgment of death upon my selfish nature and surrender all rights to my life.

3. Holy Spirit, I believe you to actually deaden me to my old nature, by your power.

4. Holy Spirit, I believe you will keep me yielded to God.

5. Holy Spirit, I ask you to make Christ Lord, the boss of my life: I trust you to arrange my schedule today. I depend upon your strength for all I do, and I now proclaim Christ Lord of my life!"

For the Spirit   *Daily Filling Instructions*

Warning: Yesterdays filling will not effect today. You must be filled daily, and hourly, as needed.

Instructions:

1. *The Thirsting.* Never pray mechanically. You must pray with intense desire!

2. *The Confessing.* Acknowledge each unconfessed sin, name it, forsake it, and ask forgiveness.

3. *The Obeying.* Report for duty. Commit yourself to obey each and every impulse of your day in order to be of service for anything God wishes to do through your life!

4. *The Asking.* Ask for the Holy Spirit's fullness.

5. *The Believing.* Depart to serve, believing you are filled.

For Besetting Sins   *Demolition Plan*

Besetting sins are oft repeated sins. They are *suckers,* latent expressions from the old nature that must be pruned. They are *snares* of the devil in our life, where Satan can entice us to sin almost at his will. Mostly, they are *Hill Sixtys,* stubborn areas of resistance to God where victory comes hardest.

The following is God's demolition plan, for the destruction of Hill Sixtys.

1. Zero in on the besetting sins of your life. List those you intend to seek victory over: _____.

2. Apply Calvary. You apply the slaying efficacy of Calvary's cross to your besetting sin by becoming dead to that sin, in the following manner. Pray:

(1) *With Yieldedness.* "Lord, I commit myself to act as you direct, in dependence upon the Holy Spirit, throughout this day. I will do as you lead, one impulse at a time."

(2) *By Reckoning.* "Now, Lord, I reckon myself dead to the sin of *(name it)* and I believe I will become nonresponsive to it."

(3) *Through the Spirit.* "Holy Spirit, I trust you to carry out the execution."

(4) *From the Heart.* "I am mentally prepared for withdrawal pains, emotionally motivated by love for you, willfully resisting with all my might!"

TRAVELER'S AIDS II

For Use in the Wilderness   *Wilderness Survival Kit*

This is a wilderness survival kit. Its faithful use will sustain you through your journey and take you through to your full spiritual inheritance.

Directions: Meet all trials with trust and move upward. List some things you will pray for in the upward progress of your life: ....

Caution: This is a wilderness kit. The children of Israel died in the wilderness from unbelief. Test all you are seeking God for and express full-hearted faith:

1. Test your mind: What do you base it on? Do you have a scriptural principle or promise as a basis for seeking this?

2. Test your emotions: Why do you want it? Do you want it primarily for God's sake?

3. Test your will: How do you express it? Have you taken an action which reveals you consider it already done?

For Strength   *Exercise Chart*

Practice abiding in Christ through all of these means:
Check yourself daily! Stay at it until it becomes habitual!

1. *Faith:* Things I am believing God for ....

2. *Scripture:* When I intend to study each day .... What I intend to study ....

3. *Holy Spirit:* When I intend to daily seek the Spirit's filling ....

4. *Love:* I am seeking to express God's love to others by faithfulness to the following activities .... and the following attitudes ....

5. *Witnessing:* Here is how I intent to witness ....
(by use of tracts, by making visits, etc.).

6. *Cleansing:* Here is when I will have my daily confession ....

7. *Obedience:* I am seeking renewed obedience in the following areas

....

8. *Prayer:* Here is when I will have my daily prayer time ....

For Satan   *Declaration of War*

Our Warfare

Battle strategy: We war from victory, not to it. Satan is a defeated foe. We exercise our authority in Christ.

Battle Tactic: "Submit yourselves therefore to God. Resist the devil, and he will flee from you" (Jas. 4:7).

Offensive weapons for submitting:

1. Yielding toward your Savior: Yield to all he wants of your life.

2. Reckoning toward yourself: Reckon yourself dead to self and besetting sins.

Defensive weapons for resisting:

1. Rejoicing through oppression: Refusing to accept circumstances as final, hold on until you can rejoice.

2. Rejecting his suggestions: Pray. Tell Jesus on him. By faith just ask for that of Christ you need to reject Satan's suggestions. Ask for faith to turn away doubtful thoughts, etc. Eject the devil when you sense his presence; command him to leave in Jesus' name.